THE EDUCATION SYSTEM TRANSFORMED

THE EDUCATION SYSTEM
TRANSFORMED
A GUIDE TO THE SCHOOL REFORMS

CLYDE CHITTY

baseline
BOOKS

First published 1992 by
Baseline Book Company
PO Box 34
Chorlton
Manchester M21 1LL

British Library Cataloguing in Publication Data

ISBN 1 897626 01 0

Cover design   Ian Price
Cover illustration   Min Cooper
Typesettting   Kathryn Holliday
Printed and bound by Nuffield Press, Oxford

CONTENTS

TABLES

ACKNOWLEDGEMENTS

Numerous friends and colleagues kindly commented on draft chapters of this book. For constant advice and encouragement I would like particularly to thank Denis Baylis, Sue Butterfield, Ian Campbell, David Crooks, Derek Gillard, Lyndon Godsall, Duncan Graham, Andy Green, Pauline Green, Gordon Kirkpatrick, Roy Lowe, Mairtin Mac an Ghaill, Linda Powell, Stewart Ranson, Peter Ribbins, Roger Seckington, Brian Simon, Jim Thawley, Hywel Thomas, David Tombs and Nanette Whitbread. I also owe a special debt to the 1991-92 PGCE students at the University of Birmingham – particularly Paul Burke, Gavin Burrows and Alan Groucott – for their helpful comments on preliminary versions of chapters which they had to endure as course materials. Special thanks are due to Jenny Neave for help with preparation of the final text. Errors which remain are, of course, my own.

Clyde Chitty
August 1992

ABBREVIATIONS

CEO	Chief Education Officer
CPS	Centre for Policy Studies
CTC	City Technology College
DES	Department of Education and Science
DFS	Department for Education
DSPU	Downing Street Policy Unit
FAS	Funding Agency for Schools
FEFC	Further Education Funding Council
FEVER	Friends of the Education Voucher Experiment in Representative Regions
GCSE	General Certificate of Secondary Education
HMI	Her Majesty's Inspectorate
IEA	Institute of Economic Affairs
IPPR	Institute for Public Policy Research
LEA	Local Education Authority
LMS	Local Management of Schools
MSC	Manpower Services Commission
NAHT	National Association of Head Teachers
NCC	National Curriculum Council
NCES	National Council for Educational Standards
NUT	National Union of Teachers
SAT	Standard Assessment Task
SCAA	School Curriculum and Assessment Authority
SEAC	School Examination and Assessment Council
TGAT	Task Group on Assessment and Testing
TVEI	Technical and Vocational Education Initiative

INTRODUCTION

Education emerged as a key issue in the 1992 general election campaign. Although it perhaps failed to arouse quite as much passion as controversy surrounding the future of the National Health Service, it was placed near the top of the political agenda by the Liberal Democrats' pledge to make a £2 billion injection into British education a condition of participation in coalition government. This high profile came at the end of more than a decade of constant and momentous change in the education system of England and Wales. It is moreover clear that change will continue to disrupt the education system as the 1990s progress.

THE REFORM AGENDA

The Conservatives under Margaret Thatcher were in some respects slow to develop a distinctive reform agenda for education. However, towards the end of the Thatcher decade the pace and radicalism of educational change increased markedly. Central to Thatcherite reform in this sphere was the Education Reform Act 1988. This was the most important and far-reaching piece of educational legislation since the Education Act 1944 (known as the Butler Act).

That the radical drive will be continued by the Major administration became clear very soon after the Conservatives' fourth successive election victory. The White Paper, *Choice and Diversity: A New Framework for Schools*, released by Education Secretary John Patten in July 1992, heralds further substantial reform of the education system in England and Wales.

The nature of that reform is, however, complex and at times difficult to understand. With terms such as 'privatisation', 'market forces' and 'grant-maintained status' being very much part of current education debate, it is indeed hardly surprising that many people – especially teachers and parents – are increasingly confused by educational issues, and worried about what the future holds in store.

This book analyses reform of education in the 1980s and 1990s, placing it in the context of educational development in the years since 1944, when the Butler Act was passed. It looks in detail at the many aspects of reform, and surveys both the state of the education system in the 1980s, and its likely development during the course of the 1990s. Finding many aspects of current education policy to be misguided, it suggests alternative ways forward.

ASPECTS OF THE REFORM PROGRAMME

The first task is, however, simply to outline the major changes that are now taking place in the education system.

- A national curriculum is gradually being introduced throughout the school system. The Education Reform Act 1988 stated that pupils aged five to sixteen must study nine subjects in primary school and ten in secondary school. (The difference is that only pupils of secondary school age are required to learn a modern foreign language.) Three of these subjects – mathematics, English and science – are called core subjects. The remaining seven – a modern foreign language, technology, history, geography, art, music and physical education – are known as foundation subjects. In Wales, schools which are in predominantly Welsh-speaking areas study Welsh as a core subject, while the rest include it as a foundation subject. Each subject in the new curriculum has been phased in gradually, starting with the youngest pupils in both primary and secondary schools. According to the Patten White Paper, some secondary schools are to be encouraged to specialise in one or a small number of subjects, in addition to offering the full national curriculum.
- A national programme of testing is being introduced, designed in part to ensure that the national curriculum is being followed properly in all schools. Pupils are assessed when they reach the end of four key stages in their school career: at the ages of 7, 11, 14 and 16. These are known in educational jargon as Key Stages One, Two, Three and Four. Assessment consists of two major elements. The first part is carried out by classroom teachers who record their pupils' progress on each aspect of the national curriculum. The second judgment is based on how pupils perform in a range of national tests. Initially these were commissioned by the School Examinations and Assessment Council (SEAC). The 1992 White Paper proposes merger of SEAC with another body created by the 1988 Act, the National Curriculum Council (NCC). Tests will then be commissioned by the new School Curriculum and Assessment Authority (SCAA). Tests were introduced for 7 year-olds in 1991. They will be taken by 14 year-olds in 1993 and by 11 year-olds in 1994.

- Changes continue to be made to the General Certificate of Secondary Education (GCSE). This, the common system of examining at 16-plus, was introduced as recently as the summer of 1988. The government is now anxious to reduce the proportion of course work in each subject that can count towards the final grade, preferring to return to a system which places more importance on examinations.

- Schools are being required to provide detailed statistical information about themselves on a wide range of issues. These statistics are known as performance indicators. Prominent among these are examination results which are increasingly being used in published league tables to show which schools in a particular locality are performing well and which badly. The *Parent's Charter* requires all schools to report to parents at least annually on the progress of their children.

- Headteachers are being made increasingly responsible for administering their own budgets by means of the local management of schools (LMS) initiative. According to Department of Education and Science (DES) circulars issued by the former Schools Minister Michael Fallon, local education authorities (LEAs) must delegate at least 85 per cent of the 'Potential Schools Budget' to individual schools by April 1993. At the same time, 80 per cent of that delegated budget must be determined strictly by the number of pupils in the school. In reality, some 70 per cent of a school's budget is likely to be devoted to teaching and non-teaching salaries and accompanying 'costs of employment' like national insurance and superannuation. Guidance from the Education Department makes it clear that in addition to salary items, delegation is expected to extend to schools' day-to-day premises costs, including rent and rates, books, equipment and other goods and services.[1]

- Alongside provisions for financial delegation, schools are now required to admit pupils to their physical capacity. Each school is given a standard number which, in effect, is the total admissions for either 1979-80 or 1989-90, whichever is the larger. The Patten White Paper also gives prominence to the government's determination to eradicate the surplus 1.5 million school places which are a current feature of the education system.

- Most controversially of all, primary and secondary schools are now being encouraged to 'opt out' of LEA control and acquire grant-maintained status. By the time of the 1992 general election, only 219 of the 25 000 schools in England and Wales had chosen to take this option. Significantly, more than 100 of these came from the 25 lowest-spending LEAs. By the end of the academic year 1991-92, this number had risen to 287. The Patten White Paper nevertheless predicts that by April 1994 there could be more than 1500 grant-maintained schools in England and Wales. As far as secondary schools are concerned, it is further predicted that at least one in ten will choose to reintroduce selection, indicating a clear return to a two-tier system of secondary schooling. However, the ironical situation has also developed whereby schools in Wandsworth and Bedfordshire plan to seek grant-maintained status in order to remain comprehensive. Contained in the 1992 White Paper was the government's decision to establish a new statutory body, the Funding Agency for Schools (FAS), to take over from the Department for Education (DFE) the payment of money to grant-maintained schools.

- By September 1993, a total of 15 city technology colleges (CTCs) will be in operation. The final two to open are in Derby (September 1992) and Bristol (September 1993). It was originally intended that there would be at least 20 CTCs in the first phase, but it has proved difficult to find suitable sponsors. Even those CTCs which have opened have attracted far less private finance than was desired by government.

- Despite the opposition of the major teacher unions, the government is committed to the introduction of appraisal for all teachers in state schools from 1992. It is intended that all teachers will have undergone an appraisal process by 1994-95.

- From April 1993, further education, sixth form and tertiary colleges are to be removed from local authority control and centrally administered through a Further Education Funding Council (FEFC).

- Building on the new encouragement to schools to plan separate academic and vocational courses for their students from at least the age of 14 (in other words, at Key Stage Four), schools and colleges are being expected to implement a divided curriculum at the post-16 stage. However, technical and vocational courses are to be accorded the same status as those leading to A-level. The government is quite determined that A-level courses should not be jettisoned.

- Her Majesty's Inspectorate (HMI) faces a severe cutback in numbers, although a degree of confusion continues to surround government plans for school inspection following the pre-election decision of the House of Lords to overturn key aspects of Kenneth Clarke's Schools Bill.

- As far as teacher training is concerned, the government has drawn up radical plans which involve a substantial switch of funding from colleges and universities to schools. In line with the new proposals, trainee secondary teachers will spend two-thirds of their training year in the classroom supervised by experienced 'mentor' teachers. Mentors will probably earn extra money for taking on this new responsibility.

THE ISSUE OF PRIVATISATION

This long list of changes, many of which encompass greater private-sector involvement in the education system, has provoked widespread debate about privatisation. Indeed, it is often claimed that the Conservatives are intent on privatising education. At the outset, it is important to be clear about what is meant by privatisation in this context.

Clearly privatisation in education is not precisely equivalent to the process whereby such public utilities as telecommunications, gas, water and electricity were sold into the private sector by the Thatcher administration. Similarly, current plans to privatise British Rail and the Royal Mail are not in all respects the same as plans to reform the education system. Yet the exact meaning of the term privatisation in the education sphere is very difficult to specify.

Both in this country and abroad, privatisation is given many different meanings. In America, it is taken to indicate a measure of independent management and diversity of provision within the state system. This is rarely the case in Britain, where emphasis is generally placed on a transfer of control from the public sector to the private. However, even here grant-maintained status is sometimes referred to as privatisation when, strictly speaking, grant-maintained schools remain within the state system.[2] Confusion is therefore possible even when debate is restricted to a single political system. In order to avoid, or at least minimise, confusion, it is best to restrict use of the term to those measures designed to produce a system within which all schools are both privately run and able to charge fees.

PRIVATISATION IN THE 1980s AND 1990s

It can be argued that in the 1980s privatisation of education assumed two major forms. The first was the purchasing at private expense of educational services which formerly were free within the public system. The second was the purchasing at public expense of educational services in private institutions.

In the 1990s a third category can be added to these two. This is privatisation in the sense of impoverishing the maintained sector to such an extent that anxious parents with money to spare feel more or less obliged to select some form of private education for their children. Indeed, it is even possible that a fourth category is emerging, in that a number of recent innovations (notably establishment of the CTC scheme) can be said to represent a gradual blurring of the boundary between state and private provision. For the purpose of introducing the topic of privatisation in the 1980s and 1990s, it is easiest to concentrate on the first two categories, leaving a fuller discussion of the third and fourth to later parts of this book.

The first category – and, as it happens, the fourth as well – includes the various ways in which parents and institutions in the private sector have been asked to pay for both essential and inessential services within the public sector. Examples are special lessons or curriculum innovations, resources and books, repairs and maintenance, basic facilities and buildings, and even teaching posts. By the middle of the 1980s, the National Confederation of Parent-Teacher Associations estimated that £40 million a year was being required of parents for aspects of education which continue to be regarded as essential: books, equipment and lessons.

Similarly, a succession of HMI reports in the 1980s catalogued the neglect of state primary and secondary schools, revealing that it had become commonplace for parents to paint and decorate classrooms in order to ensure a civilised environment for their children. These same reports pointed to the need for parents to contribute large sums of money to their children's schools in order to compensate for a desperate shortage of books and other resources. The Inspectorate noted, moreover, that private funding of education was not distributed evenly throughout the country. Schools in rich shire counties inevitably received more parental money than did their counterparts in the inner cities.

Turning to the second category, it quickly becomes apparent that most independent schools depend on financial support from the tax-payer. At present, around 7 per cent of the secondary age-group in England and Wales are educated in the private sector. For the present government this is where 'real' academic education is to be found. Benn points out that public funds – which ought by rights to be spent on state schools – are being diverted by a variety of means, both open and devious, to the independent sector. Twenty years ago, it was estimated that, on average, 20 per cent of the income of independent schools came from those who were not educated in them and who therefore did not enjoy their benefits. Since then, subsidies have escalated in cost and pro-liferated in kind, making it very difficult to arrive at an exact figure for the national yearly subsidy bill. It is certain now to be higher than the 20 per cent registered in the 1970s.[3]

Of special significance in this connection is the Assisted Places Scheme introduced by Education Secretary Mark Carlisle in 1980. This was designed to allow a privileged group of 'high ability' children to transfer from the maintained sector to selected private schools. Under the scheme, the parents of some 33 000 pupils currently receive assis-tance with private school fees on a scale linked to their incomes. The scheme thereby provides direct financial support for selected high-status private schools at a time when funding for state education is under heavy pressure. It also gives official support to the whole private sector and can be seen as indicative of a distinct lack of confidence in the quality of state education. Indeed it was described by Labour peer Lord Alexander during a House of Lords debate in September 1982 as 'an offensive pub-lic declaration by a government that the national system of education is incapable of providing for our most able children'.[4]

All of this could be said to be little more than tinkering with the system. However, the government's more extreme supporters have made no secret of their impatience with piecemeal reform and their desire to reach a situation in which all schools are owned by individual trusts. Parents would then be provided with education vouchers to spend at the school of their choice.

The first of these objectives might be difficult to achieve. It can, however, be argued that the introduction of per capita (or per pupil) funding as part of the provision for financial delegation in the 1988 legislation is, in effect, a subtle means of adapting the education system in such a way as to make a future transition to education vouchers possible without too much disruption.

The school has ceased to be 'maintained' as an institution independently of choices exercised by parents. Under new schemes for financial dele-gation, per capita payments are still paid to the school itself, but circumstances have been engineered in which it would be a relatively sim-ple matter to let the money go directly to parents instead, in the form of vouchers or warrants. At this point, the transfer of effective power from public institutions to parents would be complete.[5]

OFFICIAL DENIGRATION OF STATE SCHOOLS

These changes are, moreover, taking place against a background of official denigration of state schools and increasing government support for the private sector. April 1991 saw the first publication of a DES *Statistical Bulletin* devoted to independent schools in England. This kind of information had never been published in this series before. The decision to include it now is clearly indicative of a general blurring of the distinction between the rival systems.

Similarly, the *Parent's Charter*, first published in 1991, includes information about the private sector, and gives parents addresses to which they can write for further details about grant-maintained schools, CTCs, independent schools and the Assisted Places Scheme. As Walford has pointed out, this is probably the first time that the Independent Schools Information Service has received such free publicity in an official government document.[6]

Again, in January 1992, LEAs were more or less instructed to act as 'advertising agents' for the private sector. The information they publish for parents must now include full details of the Assisted Places Scheme and of any private schools operating in their area.

Finally, in a House of Commons debate on teachers' pay and conditions at the end of April 1991, Education Secretary Kenneth Clarke was quoted by his opposite number Jack Straw as saying approvingly in an interview published in *Woman* magazine, 'I have never met anybody who did not wish to send their children into independent education if they could afford it'.[7]

This, then, is the context in which current education debate is taking place. It is crucially important to be clear about its terms before attempting to work out how it might reshape the education system of England and Wales in the closing years of this century.

NOTES

1. Until the 1992 general election, the department with responsibility for the education system of England and Wales was known as the Department of Education and Science (DES). After the general election, responsibility for science was transferred to a new ministry, and the Department for Education (DFE) was formed.

2. Some independent schools, notably those boarding schools with declining rolls, are attempting to persuade the government to extend grant-maintained status to private schools (so that they can opt into it). This is a good example of the state system being asked to come to the rescue of establishments unable to cope with the vagaries of the market.

3. Direct and indirect subsidies were calculated at £654 million in 1980: see R Rogers, 'The Myth of Independent Schools', *New Statesman*, 4 January 1980. In 1990 this figure was updated to a minimum of £1.3 billion: see C Benn, 'The Public Price of Private Education and Privatisation', *Forum* 32 (1990), 68-73. This latter figure is clearly an under-estimate, because it takes no account of new forms of subsidy resulting from Conservative policy in the 1980s.

4. Quoted in the *Times Educational Supplement*, 19 September 1982.

5. S Maclure, *Education Re-Formed: A Guide to the Education Reform Act 1988* (Hodder and Stoughton, London, 1988).

6. G Walford, 'Privatisation in Education', *Forum* 34 (1992), autumn issue (forthcoming).

7. *Hansard*, H of C, vol 190, no 97, cols 49-50, 29 April 1991.

1 THE EDUCATION SYSTEM 1944-79

For some four decades, the education system of this country was dominated by the provisions of the Education Act 1944. This Act owed much to a recognition of the importance of education to economic advance and social welfare, and came to be regarded by many as a cornerstone of the post-war welfare state.

THE EDUCATION ACT 1944

The 1944 Act established secondary education for all pupils as an integral part of the education system. Education was, moreover, to be a continuous process beginning in the primary sector, continuing through the secondary, and culminating in further or higher education.

As evidence of the post-war commitment to education, the decision was taken to raise the school leaving age from 14 to 15. Problems of transition to the post-war world meant that implementation of this decision was slightly delayed, until 1947. Provision was also made for a further rise to 16 'as soon as the Minister is satisfied that it has become practicable'. In the event, ministerial satisfaction was not in evidence until the early 1970s. The change was implemented in 1973.

With regard to structure, the 1944 Act appeared to favour a bipartite (grammar and secondary modern) or tripartite (grammar, technical and secondary modern) system of secondary schooling, though comprehensive schools were not officially proscribed. Section 8 of the Act – which refers to provision of opportunities for all pupils 'in view of their different ages, abilities and aptitudes, and of the different periods for which they may be expected to remain at school' – was quoted in early post-war years by those anxious to prevent secondary reorganisation of a radical nature from taking place.

Such a reorganisation – along comprehensive lines – was indeed deferred for many years. Yet the very ambiguity of the wording of the Act ensured that when pressure for reform became almost irresistible in the 1960s it could be carried out by reinterpreting the existing formula. No further legislation was required.

Administratively, the 1944 Act set up what is often referred to as a 'national system, locally administered'. What this amounted to was a tri-partite 'partnership' between central government, local government and individual schools and colleges.[1] According to Bogdanor, the 'efficient secret' of the system was that no one individual participant or group of participants should enjoy a monopoly of power in the decision-making process. This, he notes, was desirable on grounds of efficiency, in that incorporation of all major interests tended to produce decisions with which all important parties agreed. It was also desirable on liberal and plu-ralist grounds. To the liberal, the education system offered a neat means of avoiding an undesirable concentration of power. To the plu-ralist, it offered a means of representing the many different interests which play a legitimate role in education. The result was that a network of pro-fessional communities developed alongside the formal relationships of the education system.[2]

DEVELOPMENT OF THE EDUCATION SYSTEM

This system survived for at least 30 years. Indeed, the first two or three decades after World War Two formed a period in which both major parties shared a core commitment to the underlying principles of the wel-fare state. These were a set of tacit assumptions which comprised a three-fold commitment to full employment, a mixed economy, and the various institutions of the welfare state itself. Among these, the education system embodied in the Butler Act featured strongly.

In the educational sphere, the general emphasis was on expansion. Remarkable increases in numbers of schools, of teachers and of students in higher education were registered in the years after World War Two. Furthermore, little policy conflict was apparent. Although Conservative governments of the 1950s were generally hostile to local experiments in comprehensive reorganisation, there is much truth in Dale's assertion that from 1954, when Sir David Eccles was appointed Minister of Education, until the 1964 general election, when the Conservatives were defeated, education policy was essentially non-partisan. When Sir Edward Boyle was in charge of education policy from 1962 to 1964, it was almost bipartisan.[3]

A number of factors contributed to the prevailing mood of optimism and consensus. Relative absence of damaging political conflict in the 1950s and early 1960s was greatly furthered not only by the general climate of expansion, but also by the availability of sufficient financial resources to ensure successful implementation of expansionist policies. At the same time, this was a period when the number of powerful interest groups in the educational sphere was fairly small. It was therefore comparatively easy to secure consensus amongst a cosily restricted network. As Bogdanor observes,

> The system of consultation worked best when only a small number of interests were involved whose rank and file were content to defer to elites, and could, therefore, be relied upon to act 'sensibly'. This process of elite accommodation reached its apogee during the post-war period when, or so it was believed, many policy decisions in education were taken over lunch at the National Liberal Club by a troika consisting of Sir William Alexander, Secretary of the Association of Education Committees, Sir Ronald Gould, the General Secretary of the National Union of Teachers, and the Permanent Secretary at the Department of Education. If these three agreed on some item of educational policy, it would, more often than not, be implemented. Such at least was the general belief; and, even if it was a caricature, it is at least significant that it was widely held.[4]

The spirit of co-operation and compromise was not broken, at least to begin with, by the Labour government's use of Circular 10/65 to promote the cause of comprehensive schooling in July 1965.[5] A number of pioneering LEAs – including Conservative ones – had already introduced comprehensive schools in their areas during the preceding 20 years. Indeed, by the time the Labour government was returned to power in 1964, such schools were educating nearly 10 per cent of secondary-school pupils in England and Wales.[6] Fenwick notes that the Labour policy of encouraging a shift to comprehensive schooling merely served to generate renewed coherence between national and local policy. Even those who were not in the forefront of the campaign for change believed Circular 10/65 to be an acceptable progression of policy.[7]

On the Conservative side, the educational philosophy of Sir Edward Boyle was an important factor in facilitating change. As Minister of Education from 1962 to 1964, he made it clear that he was broadly sympathetic to the case for comprehensive schools and was prepared to accept practical proposals for change. However, his party's record on education, and the opposition of a significant group of Conservative backbenchers, made it impossible for him to seize the initiative. Nevertheless, he was prepared to state in the 1963 Conservative pamphlet *Educational Opportunity* that,

> None of us believes in pre-war terms that children can be sharply differentiated into various types or levels of ability; and I certainly would not wish to advance the view that the tripartite system, as it is often called, should be regarded as the right and normal way of organising secondary education, compared with which everything else must be stigmatised as experimental.[8]

The foreword to the Newsom Report *Half Our Future*, issued by the Ministry of Education in 1963, shows that Boyle accepted one of the crucial arguments against a rigid system of selection at eleven-plus: that so-called intelligence could be 'acquired' and was not therefore a fixed quantity impervious to educational influence. As Boyle himself noted in this foreword, 'The essential point is that all children should have an equal opportunity of acquiring intelligence, and of developing their talents and abilities to the full'.

These sentiments were somehow typical of the radical and progressive spirit of the Sixties, a spirit which, initially at least, cut across party divisions. The decade saw a vigorous expansion of parental interest in education which expressed itself in the creation of a number of influential campaigning pressure groups. Removal of the eleven-plus straitjacket resulted in a new excitement in many primary schools which brought people from all parts of the world to look at 'progressive' primary practice. Between 1960 and 1970 the number of comprehensive schools grew from 130 to 1145, catering by the end of the decade for over 30 per cent of maintained-sector pupils. As Maurice Plaskow has observed, for those who believed in a genuine extension of educational opportunity, 'it was the best of times'.

> It is fashionable to deride the 1960s as culturally aberrant and wildly idealist. Healthy idealism may be preferable to entrenched ideology parading as pragmatism. Many of us who were active in education in the 1960s look back on a time of optimism, a spirit of shared concerns, and the beginnings of an articulation (in every sense) of an education system which would offer the greatest possible opportunities to everyone as an entitlement, not a privilege.[9]

BREAKDOWN OF CONSENSUS

Yet as the Sixties progressed, the uneasy cross-party alliance on a number of welfare issues fell apart, leaving little trace of that benign consensus on which implementation of comprehensive reform was based.

This was due, in large measure, to increasing evidence of the exposed nature of Boyle's position on the 'liberal' wing of the Conservative Party, a position which eventually became untenable as large groups of right-wing backbenchers and constituency activists mobilised against the beleaguered shadow Education Secretary.[10] It was now widely held within the Party that the Conservative government had been defeated in 1964 not simply because of internal dissensions, nor because the public had become bored with it (though there was seen to be truth in both assertions), but because it had espoused economic and social policies which were a diluted version of its opponents' ideas.

Nowhere did this appear to be more true than in the area of education. Boyle was widely identified as the main culprit. At the very least, he was a convenient scapegoat. Matters came to a head at the 1968 Conservative Party conference, where Boyle was challenged to acknowledge that his party was hopelessly divided on such issues as secondary education, grammar schools and reorganisation. His response was to make a passionate plea for moderation and consensus:

> I will join with you willingly and wholeheartedly in the fight against Socialist dogmatism wherever it rears its head. But do not ask me to oppose it with an equal and opposite Conservative dogmatism, because in education, it is dogmatism itself which is wrong.[11]

The plea was unsuccessful, and the official motion on education was defeated.

By 1969, when Boyle relinquished the post of Shadow Education Secretary, it was obvious that his largely non-partisan or even bipartisan approach had lost the support of grass-roots activists in the Conservative Party. Furthermore, it was simply no longer possible to paper over the cracks. Writing in *New Society* in May 1969, Corbett noted that by any measure – 'left versus right, consensus versus backlash, collectivists versus radicals, or just the informed versus the ignorant' – and at all levels, the Conservatives were divided on education.[12]

However, in the late 1960s, according to Corbett, the views of Boyle's many critics did not add up to 'a coherent rival philosophy'. Above all, there was a very real split on the right-wing of the Conservative Party between 'preservationists' who simply wanted to defend grammar schools, and so-called 'voucher men' who wanted to experiment with new and untried ways of organising education.

PRESERVATION VERSUS THE VOUCHER

It was 'preservationists' who dominated right-wing thinking until at least the mid-1970s. Such thinking found expression in a series of five *Black Papers* published between 1969 and 1977, which unexpectedly struck a popular chord and sold, at least at the beginning, in tens of thousands.

The first three *Black Papers* published in 1969 and 1970 were a vehicle for those Conservatives who wanted to put back the clock: to the days of formal teaching in primary schools, of high academic standards associated with a grammar school education, and of well- motivated, hard-working and essentially conservative university students.

Only in the last two *Black Papers*, published in 1975 and 1977, was support given to the introduction of educational vouchers and notions of greater scope for parental choice of school. By the mid-1970s, politics of reaction had been replaced by politics of reconstruction. The ground was being prepared for a more bitter ideological struggle between the main political parties.

THE IMPACT OF ECONOMIC CRISIS

The final factor which acted to reshape British politics and generate a climate in which right-wing ideas could flourish was economic crisis. The economic recession of 1973-75 fundamentally altered the map of British politics, and provided the necessary conditions for widespread dissemination of right-wing ideas. The OPEC oil crisis exposed all the underlying weaknesses of Keynesian social democracy, and Heath, Wilson and Callaghan all failed to breathe new life into the old system.

The post-war consensus had relied on increasing prosperity for such success as it might have had in creating a semblance of social unity. When that prosperity disintegrated, so too did consensus. As Marquand argues, the Keynesian approach to economic management, with its tacit rejection of the reality of class conflict, simply could not cope with the economic shocks and adjustment problems of the 1970s. As the post-war consensus collapsed, so the Conservative leadership sought to revive the market liberalism which had last prevailed in the nineteenth century. For its part, the Labour rank and file (though not its leadership) looked back to the 1920s and 1930s for socialist or neo-Marxist inspiration.[13]

While both major parties contained groups with radical ideas about the future direction of society, only in the Conservative Party – at least after Heath's defeat by Thatcher in February 1975 – did such groups enjoy easy access to the leadership.

NOTES

1. The third element in the partnership is sometimes identified as the organised teaching profession.
2. V Bogdanor, 'Power and Participation', *Oxford Review of Education* 5 (1979), 157-68.
3. R Dale, 'Thatcherism and Education', in J Ahier and M Flude (eds), *Contemporary Education Policy* (Croom Helm, London, 1983), 223-55.
4. Bogdanor, op cit, p.161.
5. This Circular asked LEAs to submit schemes for secondary reorganisation, based on six existing LEA patterns.
6. C Benn and B Simon, *Half Way There: Report on the British Comprehensive School Reform*, second edition (Penguin, Harmondsworth, 1972).
7. I G K Fenwick, *The Comprehensive School 1944-1970: The Politics of Secondary School Reorganisation* (Methuen, London, 1976).
8. Quoted in ibid, p.118.
9. M Plaskow, 'It Was the Best of Times', *Education* 176,5 (3 August 1990), p.90.
10. C Knight, *The Making of Tory Education Policy in Post-War Britain, 1950-1986* (Falmer Press, Lewes, 1990).
11. Quoted in A Corbett, 'The Tory Educators', *New Society*, 22 May 1969, 785-7.
12. Ibid.
13. D Marquand, *The Unprincipled Society: New Demands and Old Politics* (Jonathan Cape, London, 1988).

2 THE NEW RIGHT CHALLENGE

Following Conservative defeat in the general election of February 1974, and confirmation that the party would spend a number of years in opposition in the subsequent defeat of October 1974, the person who set out to articulate the views and aspirations of new right-wing radicals within the Conservative Party was Sir Keith Joseph. Initially, he attempted to persuade his existing leader, Edward Heath, to move away from the 'middle ground' in politics. Soon, however, it became clear that the New Right challenge required a change of leadership. Margaret Thatcher was elected in February 1975 to take over from Heath as Conservative Party leader.

THE LEFT-WING RATCHET

From April 1974, Joseph set out to persuade the party and the country of the error of its collective ways in the years since World War Two. In a long series of speeches, often given to student audiences, he articulated almost all the distinctive features of the economic and political philosophy which is now known as Thatcherism. By contrast, Thatcher herself engaged in very little theorising. She was instead a self-proclaimed conviction politician, her convictions somehow or another having survived remarkably intact the four years spent as Education Minister under Heath, when the main lines of policy flatly contradicted every one of those convictions.[1]

In an important speech to the Oxford Union in December 1975, Sir Keith argued that the major task facing the Conservative Party in opposition was to reverse what he described as 'the left-wing ratchet'. As far as he was concerned, the 'middle ground' was 'a guarantee of a left-wing ratchet' and had therefore to be abandoned.

> The middle ground is not rooted in the way of life, thought and work of the British people, not related to any vision of society, or attitude of mind, or philosophy of political action. It is simply the lowest common denominator obtained from a calculus of assumed electoral expediency, defined not by reference to popular feeling, but by splitting the difference between Labour's position and that of the Conservatives. But Labour's position, as we know, is itself arrived at by

> splitting the difference between their left and their centre. So the middle ground, at any given time, is fixed in relation to the Labour left and the Conservative centre. In other words, it is dictated by the extremists of the left.[2]

Joseph went on to argue that in the 1960s, the 'middle ground' had moved continually to the left by its own internal dynamic. This process had, moreover, had disastrous consequences for both the British economy and British society.

> It created not prosperity but crisis. Far from saving the private sector, it has gone a long way towards destroying it. Far from achieving social harmony and strengthening the centre, it has created resentments and conflict, has moved the centre of gravity of the whole labour movement to the left, strengthening the left-wing, the irreconcilables, the revolutionaries. Because we Conservatives became identified with the shifting middle ground, we were inhibited from fighting a vigorous battle of ideas; we became identified with an unworkable *status quo*; we therefore allowed the crisis of British socialism to be presented as the crisis of capitalism by default.[3]

In the 1970s, reversing the 'left-wing ratchet' meant reversing the ideological ratchet, and a number of groups had an important role to play in this process. Prominent among them were educational study groups.

EDUCATIONAL STUDY GROUPS

In August 1974, Margaret Thatcher and Sir Keith Joseph were instrumental in setting up the Centre for Policy Studies (CPS), an organisation intended to be a rival think-tank to the essentially moderate Conservative Research Department. It soon established a variety of sub-groups. Among them was an Education Study Group, which sought to develop radical solutions to current problems.

In the same year, a campaigning group was also established when Marjorie Seldon presented a motion in favour of experimental education vouchers to the annual conference of the National Council of Women. This led to the creation in December 1974 of Friends of the Education Voucher Experiment in Representative Regions (FEVER).

Furthermore, throughout the 1970s, the Institute of Economic Affairs (IEA), established as early as 1955, worked tirelessly to persuade the

Conservative Party to abandon the corporatist consensus and adopt poli-
cies based on nineteenth-century free-market anti-statism. Its
influence over the new Conservative leadership was acknowledged by
Margaret Thatcher herself when, a few months after becoming Prime
Minister, she wrote to the IEA's founder to express her appreciation of the
Institute's magnificent work in helping to create a new intellectual climate.
She was, she wrote, one of the IEA's 'strongest supporters'.[4]

THE CASE FOR THE VOUCHER

As has already been noted, the last two *Black Papers*, published in
1975 and 1977, went further than ever before in delineating a distinctive
right-wing agenda for education. The new emphasis was on choice, competition and parental control of schools.

It was argued that progress towards privatisation of the education system
could be achieved by gradual introduction of the voucher, a device for
establishing consumer sovereignty in education. It was based on the simple principle that all parents should be issued with a free basic
coupon, fixed at the average cost of schooling in their LEA area.

Black Paper 1975 contained a piece by the editors urging introduction of
the educational voucher in at least two trial areas, and a special essay by
Rhodes Boyson, former head teacher and by 1975 a prominent
Conservative MP, on 'The Developing Case for the Educational
Voucher'. Support for the voucher was reiterated in the editorial intro-
duction to *Black Paper 1977* which took the form of a 'Letter to
Members of Parliament':

> The possibilities for parental choice of secondary (and primary)
> schools should be improved via the introduction of the educational
> voucher or some other method. Schools that few wish to attend
> should be closed and their staff dispersed.[5]

Indeed, Boyson was a key figure in the bid to translate right-wing
educational ideas into practical policy options, being a leading member
of the National Council for Educational Standards (NCES). This body was
established in 1972 to campaign against 'progressive' teaching methods.
With his ability to command the attention of the media, Boyson acted as
an important link between the *Black Papers* and NCES on the one
hand, and Conservative Party activists on the other. He published

Battle Lines for Education (1973) and *Parental Choice* (1975) through the Conservative Political Centre. In 1975 he also published *The Crisis in Education*, in which he outlined themes which were to become familiar in the 1980s:

> The malaise in schools in Britain has followed from a breakdown in accepted curriculum and traditional values. There was little concern about either political control or parental choice so long as there was an 'understood' curriculum, which was followed by every school. Schools may have differed in efficiency, but their common values or curriculum were broadly acceptable. The present disillusionment of parents arises from their resentment that their children's education now depends upon the lottery of the school to which they are directed. Standards decline because both measurement and comparisons are impossible when aims and curriculum become widely divergent.... These problems can be solved only by making schools again accountable to some authority outside them. The necessary sanction is either a nationally enforced curriculum or parental choice or a combination of both.[6]

LABOUR IN RETREAT

The Labour Party was thrown on the defensive by the ferocity and scale of the right-wing attack on policies pursued by it in government. The leadership appeared to be acutely embarrassed by association of the party in the eyes of the public with so-called progressive education, characterised as it often was by a child-centred approach to teaching, informal pedagogic and assessment methods, and a general antipathy to hierarchy and inequality.

There was, therefore, some justification for Boyson's triumphant claim at an NCES meeting held in London in May 1976, that 'The forces of the Right in education are on the offensive. The blood is flowing from the other side now.'[7] Each Education Secretary in the 1974-79 Labour administration was distinctly half-hearted in defence of comprehensive schooling and of the new advances in primary-school teaching made possible by abolition of eleven-plus selection. Furthermore, they all seemed to work on the assumption that what they were engaged in was largely a damage limitation exercise fought on Conservative terms.

In particular, the important speech that Prime Minister James Callaghan delivered at Ruskin College, Oxford in October 1976 singularly failed to celebrate the achievements of the state education system. Opening, in Callaghan's words, a Great Debate on education, it can be seen, in part at least, as an attempt to wrest the populist mantle from the Conservative opposition and pander to perceived public disquiet at the alleged decline in educational standards. The means by which it sought to do this involved construction of a new educational consensus built around more central control of the school curriculum, greater teacher accountability and direct subordination of the secondary curriculum to the 'needs' of the economy.

In the event, the new consensus that Labour tried to construct lasted little more than ten years. Indeed, if Margaret Thatcher's own right-wing supporters had had their way, it would have disintegrated possibly as early as 1979, and certainly in 1982 when the campaign for the voucher reached its peak. However, to begin with at least, the education policy of the Conservative government elected in that year lacked radical vision and was marked by a remarkable degree of caution in the application of free-market principles. Even the voucher was to fail in the early years of Thatcherism in power.

NOTES

1. H Young, *One of Us: A Biography of Margaret Thatcher* (Macmillan, London, 1989).
2. K Joseph, *Stranded on the Middle Ground? Reflections on Circumstances and Policies* (Centre for Policy Studies, London, 1976), p.21.
3. Ibid, p.25.
4. Quoted in Knight, op cit, p.144.
5. C B Cox and R Boyson (eds), *Black Paper 1977* (Maurice Temple Smith, London, 1977), p.9.
6. R Boyson, *The Crisis in Education* (Woburn Press, London, 1975), p.141.
7. Reported in the *Times Educational Supplement*, 21 May 1976.

3 THE CAMPAIGN FOR THE VOUCHER

The New Right had good cause to expect that the sizeable Conservative victory in the 1979 general election, and the later arrival of Sir Keith Joseph at the DES in September 1981, would provide official backing for a variety of measures designed to achieve steady privatisation of the education system. In the event, its expectations proved to be misplaced.

INTELLECTUAL ATTRACTION TO THE VOUCHER

Sir Keith's predecessor at the DES, Mark Carlisle, did very little to promote radical educational initiative during his two years as Secretary of State. The single exception was the Assisted Places Scheme, introduced by means of the Education Act 1980. This scheme was designed, in the words of the 1979 Conservative Party manifesto, to enable 'less well-off parents to be able to claim part or all of the fees at certain [private] schools from a special government fund'.[1] It was very much the brainchild of Stuart Sexton, then Special Adviser to Carlisle, subsequently adviser to Joseph, and currently Director of the IEA's Education Unit.[2]

On arrival in office, Sir Keith quickly made clear his willingness to consider radical ideas. Such willingness was, moreover, popular with the Conservative rank and file. At the 1981 Conservative Party conference, Joseph received spontaneous applause when he appeared to give qualified support to the idea of introducing education vouchers as a means of increasing parental choice of school:

> I personally have been intellectually attracted to the idea of seeing whether eventually, *eventually*, a voucher *might* be a way of increasing parental choice... I know that there are very great difficulties in making a voucher deliver – in a way that would commend itself to us – more choice than the 1980 Act will, in fact, deliver. It is now up to the advocates of such a possibility to study the difficulties – and there are real difficulties – and then see whether they can develop proposals which will really cope with them.[3]

In November 1981, two right-wing pressure groups took up the challenge. The NCES and FEVER wrote to Sir Keith asking for details of problems that would need to be resolved before an education voucher scheme could be defined, and its implications for education policy assessed. A paper on the difficulties associated with a voucher scheme, prepared by Joseph's civil servants, was sent to FEVER in December 1981, with a covering letter from Sir Keith himself. In this letter, Joseph reiterated his intellectual attraction to the idea of the voucher, seeing in it a means both to extend choice and to improve standards.

Yet the memorandum itself was not sympathetic to the concept of vouchers. In its first paragraph it stated categorically that 'the Secretary of State for Education and Science has made it clear that he has no plans for the general introduction of a voucher scheme'.[4] It also provided clear evidence that civil servants at the DES were very anxious to see the whole idea quietly dropped. Indeed, those civil servants had already in fact decided that nothing in FEVER's response would be sufficiently compelling to make vouchers a desirable option.[5]

Despite opposition within the DES, Sir Keith himself continued to give tentative public backing to the voucher concept. Questioned after a speech to the Institute of Directors in March 1982 as to how far the government was prepared to go in promoting parental choice by means of a nationwide voucher system, he again reaffirmed his intellectual interest in the voucher. However, he refused to commit the government to its introduction. After further questioning from members of his audience, Sir Keith went on to defend the voucher as a 'noble idea' because it would extend parental choice.[6] At the 1982 Conservative Party conference, he argued that introduction of a voucher system would lead to a general improvement in standards through generating the discipline of competition within the education system. Yet within a year, the idea of the voucher, in pure form at least, was dead.

Why, then, did it fail? Why was Sir Keith unable to satisfy his erstwhile supporters in New Right pressure groups? Why, above all, was this the one major occasion in the 1980s when DES civil servants would appear to have defeated the government's political advisers?

DEFEAT OF THE VOUCHER

The voucher failed for a number of reasons. In the first place, it was obvious to most objective observers that the basic concept of the voucher was not as uncomplicated as might at first appear to be the case. In fact, its proponents seemed anxious to ignore rather too many questions which had never received satisfactory answers.

What would happen, for example, if a number of popular schools found themselves seriously over-subscribed? They might be able to expand, by adding mobile classrooms and employing more teachers. However, this would risk destroying, or at the very least changing, the very ethos and character which had made them popular in the first place.

Alternatively, they might decide to charge fees, and ask parents to supplement the basic voucher out of their own pocket. Yet this would mean that the theory of parental choice would be a reality only for those with the necessary income to make that choice effective. The gap between schools, particularly at the secondary level, would actually widen as the most popular ones gained extra income which could be used both to purchase additional resources, and to attract talented teachers through higher salaries. All of this would simply create a formidable hierarchy of schools.

While Sir Keith may not himself have been deterred by the prospect of a move towards greater inequality in educational provision, he was nonetheless reluctant to proceed without the support of his civil servants. Indeed, it has even been suggested that he may have been at least partially convinced by arguments they were able to muster.[7] Joseph's cerebral approach demanded coherent solutions that would stand up. He was also plainly alarmed by the discovery that implementing a new voucher system would not be as straightforward as he had imagined.[8]

The chief concerns were financial and administrative rather than ideological. What evidence there was pointed clearly to the fact that voucher schemes were costly to operate. Having gained some publicity through a BBC Television *Open Door* programme, broadcast in 1976, FEVER had managed to persuade Kent County Council to undertake a voucher feasibility study in 1977-78. The findings had revealed that whether the scheme encompassed LEA schools alone, or also included fee-paying schools, administrative costs were enormous. They ranged from £100 000 to £600 000 in the former case, and from £870 000 to £1.3 million in the latter. Moreover, these figures applied to the Ashford area alone.[9] At the same time, a voucher scheme operating in Alum Rock, California, had collapsed, unable to cope with the alarming increase in transfers between schools that the experiment had facilitated.

These bleak experiences were confirmed by the findings of Sir Keith's own civil servants, who managed to persuade him that the cost of inaugurating a voucher scheme, on either a local or a national basis, would be hard to justify to a highly sceptical public, particularly at a time of stretched resources.

By the end of 1983, the voucher had therefore been dropped. Speaking at the 1983 Conservative Party conference, Sir Keith announced that 'the voucher, at least in the foreseeable future, is dead'. He reaffirmed this in a written statement to the House of Commons in June 1984, in which he emphasised the great practical difficulties involved in making a voucher system work. The chief problem was that it would clearly be very hard to make any voucher system compatible with the statutory requirement that compulsory schooling of an acceptable standard be available to all without charge.

WHOSE VICTORY?

At the time, unexpected abandonment of the education voucher (temporary or otherwise) was seen by many as something of a victory for conservative forces at the heart of the political establishment. It seemed that the Thatcher government was not ready in 1982-83 to risk alienating a large number of its traditional supporters. Self-made individuals who had captured the Conservative Party, both at local and at national level, were apparently not yet strong enough to proceed with the next stage of their formidable programme: the breaking of the chains of collectivism. Politics of reconstruction gave way to politics of caution.

Reviewing the government's second term on 13 January 1986, the *Daily Telegraph* argued that on measures such as education vouchers, students loans and rent control repeal, Margaret Thatcher had been defeated by the political establishment. Earlier, on the BBC2 programme, *Decision-Making in Britain*, broadcast in March 1983, FEVER chairperson, Marjorie Seldon, had put the failure of education vouchers down to a lack of political will, but the basic point was similar. This view was echoed by her husband, Arthur Seldon, one-time IEA Editorial Director, who argued in 1986 that the reason for Sir Keith Joseph's regrettable decision was 'not administrative impracticability, but official feet-dragging, and political underestimation of potential popular acclaim'.[10]

However, a further factor, which is often overlooked in assessments of Sir Keith Joseph's period as Education Secretary, is necessary to a full explanation of abandonment of the voucher. This is the extent to which Sir Keith himself came under the influence of a group of politicians and industrialists often referred to as Conservative Modernisers.[11] This group became particularly influential when David (now Lord) Young was chairperson of the Manpower Services Commission (MSC) between 1982 and 1984. In this period Conservative Modernisers succeeded in giving the Education Secretary a new set of priorities.

Their main aim was to see the school curriculum – particularly at secondary school level – restructured, in order to prepare pupils for the 'world of work'. Their main achievement in the area of curriculum initiative was probably the Technical and Vocational Education Initiative (TVEI), which was introduced as a series of 14 pilot projects in a number of carefully selected schools in the autumn of 1983. By 1986, it involved 65 000 students in 600 institutions working on four-year programmes designed to stimulate work-related education, make the curriculum more relevant to post-school life, and enable students to aim for nationally-recognised qualifications in a wide range of technical and vocational subject areas. Significantly, TVEI was not a DES policy initiative, but emanated from Young's MSC.

Unlike proponents of the education voucher, Conservative Modernisers saw no particular virtue in measures designed to privatise the system. Unlike members of some right-wing campaigning groups, they had little time for the grammar school tradition which, in their view, could be held chiefly responsible for Britain's long industrial decline. Instead, they particularly admired the tripartite system of secondary schools operating in West Germany, and saw Britain's future in terms of a strictly differentiated secondary curriculum preparing pupils according to their supposed ability for the varying tasks to be performed in a modern industrial economy.

Their vision of the ideal system of education and training was neatly summarised by Lord Young in September 1985:

> My idea is that... there is a world in which 15 per cent of our young go into higher education... roughly the same proportion as now. Another 30 to 35 per cent will stay on after 16 doing the TVEI, along with other courses, and then ending up with a mixture of vocational and academic qualifications and skills. The remainder, about half, will simply go on to a two-year YTS [Youth Training Scheme].[12]

The influence of this more pragmatic and businesslike approach on the education policies pursued during Joseph's period at the DES helps to explain defeat of the voucher.

THE CAMPAIGN REVIVED

Despite opposition from a large body of Conservative opinion, campaigners for the education voucher were not, however, prepared to accept defeat. In 1986, the IEA published *The Riddle of the Voucher*, which included suggestions for half-way houses and stepping-stones. These comprised changes in the way in which education is managed which fall short of a fully-fledged voucher system, but might nevertheless pave the way for introduction of such a system later on.

It could in fact be argued that passage of the Education Reform Act 1988 secured for these right-wing campaigners a belated, if partial, victory. This, indeed, is one of the major questions considered in the next chapter. If correct, it means that in the late 1980s the New Right was able to achieve by subtle means the very objectives that had been considered politically suicidal less than a decade before, and that had apparently been defeated only a few years earlier.

NOTES

1. Conservative Party, *The Conservative Manifesto* (Conservative Central Office, London, 1979).
2. See Knight, op cit.
3. Quoted in C Chitty, *Towards a New Education System: The Victory of the New Right?* (Falmer Press, Lewes, 1989), p.183. One aim of the Education Act 1980 was to increase parental choice among state schools. However, LEAs kept the right to frustrate a parent's choice 'if the provision of efficient education or the efficient use of resources is prejudiced'.
4. Deaprtment of Education and Science, *Memorandum on Education Vouchers* (HMSO, London, 1981), p.1.
5. DES hostility towards vouchers is clear from an Open University programme, *Decision-Making in Britain*, first shown on BBC2 in March 1983.
6. K Joseph, speech to the Institute of Directors, March 1982; reprinted in a supplement to the *Director*, May 1982, 3-5.
7. See P Wilby, 'Close Up: Kenneth Baker', *Marxism Today*, April 1987.
8. See Knight, op cit.
9. Kent County Council Education Department, *Education Vouchers in Kent: A Feasibility Study* (KCC, 1978). See also C Griggs, 'The New Right and English Secondary Education', in R Lowe (ed), *The Changing Secondary School* (Falmer Press, Lewes, 1989), 99-128.
10. A Seldon, *The Riddle of the Voucher: An Inquiry into the Obstacles to Introducing Choice and Competition into State Schools* (Institute of Economic Affairs, London, 1986), p.97.
11. See K Jones, *Right Turn: The Conservative Revolution in Education* (Hutchinson Radius, London, 1989).
12. Reported in the *Times*, 4 September 1985.

4 THE EDUCATION REFORM ACT 1988

Conservative reform of the education system in the 1980s was embodied chiefly in the Education Reform Act 1988. This landmark piece of legislation represented the first substantial challenge to the system constructed at the end of World War Two, introducing to it such concepts as a national curriculum, local management of schools, grant-maintained status and city technology colleges. It has significantly altered the education system of England and Wales.

INTELLECTUAL ORIGINS OF THE ACT

By the beginning of 1987, three groups on the right wing of the Conservative Party were exerting a powerful influence on the formulation of education policy. One was the IEA, which in 1986 established its own Education Unit under Stuart Sexton (former adviser to the Conservative Party in opposition and in government). Another was the CPS, founded by Sir Keith Joseph, Margaret Thatcher and Alfred Sherman in 1974. The third was the Hillgate Group, which included among its membership leaders of the 1970s campaign for a return to traditional educational values (such as Caroline Cox), as well as more recent converts to the cause (such as Jessica Douglas-Home, John Marks, Lawrence Norcross and Roger Scruton). This group began to publish manifestos and pamphlets at the end of 1986.

It is difficult to determine the precise influence of each of these groups on education policy development in the late 1980s. However, variations of the ideas which eventually found their way into the 1987 Education Bill can be discovered in, for example, *The Riddle of the Voucher* (published by the IEA in February 1986), *Our Schools: A Radical Policy* (written by Stuart Sexton and published by the IEA's Education Unit in March 1987), and *Whose Schools? A Radical Manifesto* (issued by the newly-formed Hillgate Group in December 1986). Furthermore, after a meeting with the Education Study Group of the CPS, held in the House of Lords in spring 1987, Education Secretary Kenneth Baker remarked to his chief political adviser, 'these are the people who are setting the educational agenda'.[1]

Yet these groups are just three examples – though possibly the most prestigious and influential – of an extraordinary array of right-wing organisations and education study groups which sprang up in the 1970s and 1980s boasting impressive titles and interlocking memberships.[2] With the prospect of an imminent general election serving to concentrate their thinking, these groups all agreed early in 1987 on the need both to undermine the powers of LEAs and to establish something resembling a free market in education. They also placed tremendous emphasis on their role as Margaret Thatcher's leading intellectual supporters.

According to Scruton,

> The Conservative Party for many years tried to limp along without having an attendant halo of intellect – unlike the Labour Party which has always been able to draw on people who have been saying things more radical and more explicit than itself... I think a political party very much needs people who are saying things not because they are politically possible, but because they think they are true, which will then define the issues and give them the language with which to discuss them... In so far as people like myself and Caroline Cox and so on have any influence, that's the sort of influence it is... writing things, publishing things – which give a certain language and tone to the debate, define ultimate goals and give analysis of the situation, which I should imagine the Conservative Party can then pick and choose a bit from.[3]

The campaign for the education voucher had apparently suffered a terminal setback in 1983. However, the departure of Sir Keith Joseph from the DES in May 1986 gave Scruton and his allies the new opportunity they had been waiting for to influence the policy-making process.

NEW WAYS FORWARD

A series of educational planning meetings was held in Downing Street in 1986 and 1987. At least to begin with, the chief concern of discussants was to devise practical ways of both breaking up the comprehensive system of secondary schooling and, at the same time, overturning the concept of a 'national system, locally administered'.

For members of the Hillgate Group, the ultimate objective was a system in which all schools would be owned by individual trusts, their survival depending on their ability to satisfy customers.[4] However, it was accepted that it would be difficult to move directly towards this privatised system of schooling. In these circumstances, it was important to find ways of gradually reaching this goal over the lifetime of another parliament.

Sexton too, in his 1987 IEA pamphlet, *Our Schools*, acknowledged that the New Right had tried to move too quickly in the 1980s:

> In pursuit of the 'privatisation' of management, if not of ownership also, the mistake has been to assume that we can get from where we are now to where we want to be in one giant stride, and all in a couple of years... After a hundred years of state-managed education, it will take more time to accommodate the schools, the teachers, and, above all, the parents themselves, to a system of 'free choice': from a producer-led system to a consumer-led system, which is what it ought to be... Vouchers, or 'education credits' to use a better term, available for every child and usable at any registered school, should be the ultimate objective. That would probably take five years to achieve if a series of measures began to be introduced now, each being a positive constructive step towards that ultimate objective.[5]

The measures Sexton had in mind included creation of new types of school at the secondary level, and introduction of a system of per capita funding as stage one of a phased introduction of an education credit system.

TENSIONS SURROUNDING THE NATIONAL CURRICULUM

The one issue on which the various groups failed to reach agreement was the desirability or otherwise of a centrally-imposed national curriculum. Indeed, this source of conflict can be shown to reflect a major paradox within Thatcherism itself. As has often been pointed out, what makes New Right philosophy special is its quite unique combination of a traditional liberal defence of the free economy with a traditional conservative defence of state authority.[6]

This combination of potentially opposing doctrines means that the New Right can appear by turns libertarian and authoritarian, populist and elitist. For neo-liberals, the emphasis is always on freedom of choice, the individual, the market, minimal government, and *laissez-faire*. Neo-conservatism, by contrast, prioritises notions of social authoritarianism, the disciplined society, hierarchy, subordination, the nation and strong government. Joseph, Sexton and Sherman could be said to be leading figures on the neo-liberal wing of the movement. The leading exponent of neo- conservatism is probably Scruton.

In his book, *The Meaning of Conservatism*, first published in 1980, Scruton describes the philosophy of liberalism, particularly when it is applied to non-economic issues, as 'the principal enemy of conservatism'. Indeed, he denounces all 'liberal' notions of 'individual autonomy' and the concept of 'natural rights of man'. In his view, a genuine conservative attitude is one which:

> seeks above all for government, and regards no citizen as possessed of a natural right that transcends his obligation to be ruled. Even democracy – which corresponds neither to the natural nor to the supernatural yearnings of the normal citizen – can be discarded without detriment to the civil well-being, as the Conservative conceives it.[7]

In the education sphere, it was the Hillgate Group, of which Scruton was a leading member, which urged introduction of a detailed national curriculum for all pupils. Such a curriculum would, in its scheme of things, uphold traditional educational values and instil respect for the family, the church, private property and all bodies charged with maintaining the authority of the state. It would preach the moral virtue of free enterprise and the pursuit of profit, a concept designed to appeal to the IEA and, indeed, the Prime Minister herself.

Yet in the course of heated debate, even this aspect of the proposed curriculum framework failed to win the support of neo-liberals. Discussing on a BBC *Panorama* programme broadcast in November 1987 the education planning which had taken place in Downing Street earlier in the year, Sexton made it clear that he and others had remained totally opposed to the idea of a government-imposed curriculum. There was general support for the Hillgate Group's special emphasis on morality and social order, but it was felt that a return to traditional values could be achieved quite easily by imposition merely of a fairly limited compulsory core. On one occasion, according to Sexton, Prime Minister Margaret Thatcher had said that her chief concern was 'the teaching of the 6Rs: reading, writing, arithmetic, religious education and right and wrong'. This would constitute her limited compulsory core curriculum for both primary and secondary schools.

It was largely the new Education Secretary, Kenneth Baker, and a number of influential DES civil servants who found a way of winning the support of at least some neo-liberals for the concept of central control of the curriculum.[8] It was possible, they found, to argue that in one major respect a national curriculum was not necessarily incompatible with free market principles. It would, after all, act as justification for a massive programme of national testing at important stages in a child's school career, thereby providing crucial evidence to parents of the desirability or otherwise of individual schools. In other words, additional consumer information provided by test results would actually facilitate operation of a market system.

THE DECISION TO EMBARK ON MAJOR REFORM

The intellectual background to the Education Reform Act 1988 was therefore complex. The Conservative Party's decision to make educational change an important part of its programme for a third term in government was based on the realisation that comparatively little had been done in the previous eight years to shake up the educational establishment.

Education was, then, one area in which Thatcherite principles had not yet been actively applied. As Foreign Secretary Sir Geoffrey Howe noted in a speech to Conservatives in the City of London at the beginning of June 1988,

> The new frontier of Conservatism – or, rather, the later stage in that rolling frontier – is about reforming those parts of the state sector which privatisation has so far left largely untouched: those activities in society such as health and education which together consume a third of our national income, but where market opportunities are still hardly known.[9]

After leaving office, Joseph himself admitted that not enough had been done in the social arena to promote the Thatcherite project. In particular, the frontiers of choice had not been extended far enough in the sphere of education.[10]

This view had indeed been foreshadowed in pre-election statements by the Prime Minister herself. In an interview with the editor of the *Daily Mail* on 13 May 1987, Margaret Thatcher had said,

> We are going much further with education than we ever thought of doing before. When we've spent all that money per pupil, and even with more teachers, there is still so much wrong; so we are going to do

something determined about it... There is going to be a revolution in the running of the schools.

Asked, by a caller to a pre-election radio and television programme broadcast on 10 June 1987, what she regretted she had not been able to achieve during eight years of Conservative government, Thatcher replied,

> In some ways, I wish we had begun to tackle education earlier. We have been content to continue the policies of our predecessors. But now we have much worse left-wing Labour authorities than we have ever had before – so something simply has to be done.

That 'something' turned out to be the most comprehensive piece of educational legislation since the Butler Act of 1944.

MAJOR PROVISIONS OF THE ACT

The Education Reform Act 1988 was intended to erect (or, perhaps more accurately, reinforce) a hierarchical system of schooling (particularly at the secondary level) subject both to market forces and to greater control by central government. For the purposes of this chapter, it is best to concentrate on three major changes affecting schools which result from the legislation.

The first of these is introduction of a national curriculum for all state schools alongside a national system of assessment for pupils aged from five to sixteen years. The 1988 Act defined mathematics, English and science as core subjects, with a second group as foundation subjects: a modern foreign language (though not for primary-school children), technology, history, geography, art, music and physical education. During passage of the Education Bill through parliament in 1987-88, religious education was added to these ten subjects as the one and only basic subject.

For most subjects the Act stated that there would be attainment targets for children aged 7, 11, 14 and 16. These would, moreover, provide standards against which pupils' progress and performance could be assessed. It was originally envisaged that much of the assessment would be undertaken by teachers as an integral part of normal classroom work. However, in the words of the 1987 National Curriculum

Consultation Document published by the DES, 'at the heart of the assessment process, there will be nationally prescribed tests done by all pupils to supplement the individual teachers' assessments'.[11]

The second major change is introduction of a system of school management known as local management of schools. LMS is the change which has many features of an educational voucher scheme. School budgets for staffing, premises and services were now to be delegated to individual schools. The delegated budget itself would be determined by a formula largely reflecting the number of pupils on a school roll. Accompanying this change was an alteration to admissions regulations which meant that schools in future would be obliged to admit pupils to their full capacity.

The third major change is creation of a new tier of schooling comprising city technology colleges and grant-maintained schools. The CTC plan, announced previously by Kenneth Baker in a speech to the 1986 Conservative Party conference, envisaged the establishment of around 20 schools for 11-18 year-olds. Each was to be financed partly by the private sector, to be independent of LEA control, and to be sited with the prime purpose of providing a new choice of secondary school for inner-city pupils. Grant-maintained schools were to be those which chose to opt out of the locally maintained education system, and to receive instead direct funding from central government. The 1988 Act allowed the governors of all secondary schools, and of primary schools with more than 300 registered pupils, to apply to the Secretary of State for grant-maintained status.

These, then, were three of the most far-reaching changes introduced by the 1988 Act. With its 238 clauses and 13 schedules, it received the royal assent on 29 July 1988. It was described by Peter Wilby and Ngaio Crequer in the *Independent* of 28 July 1988 as 'a Gothic monstrosity of legislation'. It increased the powers of the Education Secretary to a quite alarming degree, and restored to central government a control over the school curriculum which had been surrendered in the inter-war period. While gathering more power to the centre, it simultaneously introduced important limitations on the functions of LEAs, who were forced to give greater autonomy to schools, heads and governing bodies. Above all, it effectively ended that ill-defined partnership between central government, local government and individual schools which had been such a prominent feature of the educational scene since the settlement of 1944.

INTERPRETATIONS OF THE ACT

It is possible to view the 1988 Act – and the 1987 Bill from which it emerged – in a number of ways. As far as the Thatcher government was concerned, it was primarily an attempt to raise educational standards and to extend parental choice. These were the objectives cited by Education Secretary Kenneth Baker when he spoke in defence of his Bill to the House of Commons in December 1987:

> Our education system has operated over the past forty years on the basis of the framework laid down by Rab Butler's 1944 Act, which, in turn, built on the Balfour Act of 1902. We need to inject a new vitality into that system. It has become producer-dominated. It has not proved sensitive to the demands for change that have become ever more urgent over the past ten years. This Bill will create a new framework, which will raise standards, extend choice, and produce a better-educated Britain.[12]

Baker had indeed been keen to emphasise the importance of differentiation and choice in an interview with Stuart Maclure published by the *Times Educational Supplement* on 3 April 1987:

> I want a much greater degree of variety and independence in the running of schools. I do want to see a greater amount of variety and choice... What we have at present is seven per cent or so in the independent sector, probably going to rise to ten per cent; and on the other side a huge continent: 93 per cent in the state-maintained sector. I'm responsible for that state sector. What I think is striking in the British education system is that there is *nothing in between*... Now the City Technology Colleges are a sort of half-way house. I would like to see many more half-way houses, a greater choice, a greater variety. I think many parents would as well.

Others saw the Act as being intended primarily to challenge the producer interest in education (an issue touched upon by the Education Secretary in his House of Commons statement quoted above) and to make the education service more accountable for its performance. Indeed, it could be argued that over the previous decade or so, accountability had already replaced partnership as the dominant metaphor in educational discourse.[13] According to Nick Stuart, Deputy Secretary at the DES and the man chiefly responsible for drafting the final version of the 1988 Act, 'accountability has been regarded by the Conservative Government as the linchpin of its education reforms'. In his view, the legislation was essentially about three things:

provision of an improved basic curriculum for schools; extension of parental choice and influence; and better management of institutions. He further argued that notions of accountability were the link between these three.[14]

For Sexton, this search for better management of schools was one of the central reasons for the 1988 Act. Writing in the *Sunday Times* on 22 April 1990, he argued that:

> Effective management of schools was, and remains, the central theme of the Education Reform Act... If we could only restore effective management to school level, a great bonus would be that the immense resources being put into education would be more effectively used... to the benefit of the children and high standards of education... The core of the 1988 Act is all those measures giving schools within the state system both the freedom and the incentive to manage more effectively.

Those less favourably disposed towards the 1988 Act have seen a more malign purpose in it. It has, for example, been viewed as an attempt to circumvent and undermine comprehensive education through both creation of new types of school and encouragement of greater differentiation within comprehensive systems (by means of open entry and LMS).[15] Indeed, in earlier years the Thatcher administration had been anxious to encourage reintroduction of eleven-plus selection and restoration of grammar school status wherever it had been felt local support could be guaranteed. However, the two LEAs which had actually attempted to put the clock back – Solihull and Redbridge – had both failed to do so, largely as a result of enormous parental opposition. As Shadow Education Secretary Jack Straw pointed out in the *Sunday Correspondent* of 22 July 1990,

> The meretricious agenda of the 1988 Education Reform Act is in many ways a tribute to the resilience of the comprehensive ideal. Devices like opting-out, open admission, CTCs and the introduction of 'local markets' are attempts to introduce selection *by the back door.*

The 1988 Act has also been seen as an attempt to undermine – and eventually destroy – the power and influence of LEAs. Writing in the *Independent* on election day (11 June) 1987, education correspondent Peter Wilby forecast that, 'the return of a Conservative government today will mean the break-up of the state education system that has existed since 1944'. He might more accurately have predicted an end to the state system, locally administered, for it is local administration which is undermined by the 1988 Act.

The New Right has certainly never made any secret of its contempt for locally-controlled education systems, regarding their abolition as an essential first step on the road to complete privatisation. Kenneth Baker's speech to the 1986 Conservative Party conference received sustained and rapturous applause at the point at which he announced that the new CTCs would be completely independent of LEA control. In an interview with the *Independent* published on 14 September 1987, Thatcher looked forward to a situation in which 'most schools' would have chosen to opt out of LEA control and become, in her words, 'independent state schools'. The Hillgate Group argued in 1986 that, apart from any other considerations, if children were to be taught decent moral values, 'the politicised local education authorities must be deprived of their major source of power and of their standing ability to corrupt the minds and souls of the young'.[16]

In Simon's view, the main thrust of all the government's legislative reforms has been towards 'destabilising locally controlled "systems" and, concomitantly, pushing the whole structure of schooling towards a degree, at least, of privatisation, so establishing a base which can be further exploited later'.[17] According to Thomas, the conditions for what is virtually a voucher system already exist in the provisions of the 1988 Act.

Indeed, Thomas has consistently argued that financial delegation, formula funding, open enrolment, new regulations creating the prospect of redundancy for staff in schools which lose pupils, and the development of performance indicators for schools together constitute a sort of pupil-as-voucher scheme. Schools which are perceived as 'successful' will attract more pupils. They will therefore receive more funds, and will be able to appoint staff of their choice. By contrast, those schools which do not enjoy a high reputation will attract fewer pupils, less money and will probably need to dismiss staff. In this way, many establishments may be allowed to wither and die.[18]

It is in this sense that the apparently failed campaign for the voucher in the early 1980s may in fact have succeeded by more subtle means later in that same decade.

TENSIONS AND CONTRADICTIONS

Twenty years ago, the radical Right constituted a number of small, marginalised pressure groups, divided in their aims and viewed with a mixture of indifference and contempt by most members of the political establishment. By the end of the 1980s, the educational off-shoots of these groups were strong enough to impose their will on the DES. Their ideas and policies came to dominate the educational agenda to such an extent that many began to fear that any defence of the old orthodoxies would henceforth be little more than an exercise in damage limitation fought on the radical Right's terms. As Brown observed in 1989,

> Those in the Centre and on the Left in British political and academic life have much to learn from their right-wing opponents about political lobbying, the manipulation of the media, and forming political alliances, not to mention an ability to 'think the unthinkable'.[19]

Yet, as has been noted here, it would be wrong to exaggerate the coherent nature of radical or New Right philosophy, or the extent to which Margaret Thatcher and her allies succeeded in attracting widespread popular support for many of their more extreme ideas.

Indeed, it can be argued that Thatcherism in its heyday was an uneasy attempt to link the principles of a free-market economy with an atavistic emphasis on the family, traditional moral values and the virtues of a strong state. It involved rolling back the frontiers of the state in some areas, while pursuing policies of repression and coercion in others. There was a marked hostility to all institutions which mediated between the individual and the state, so that the state would emerge as the only collectivity in a society of individuals.

Civil society was seen to be composed – almost exclusively – of economically rational individuals freely pursuing their own self-interest, with minimum concern for fellow citizens. In the new order of things, men and women were to be reduced to their market value. This meant that if you had nothing, it automatically followed that you were nothing. The rhetoric of Thatcherism may have been that of choice and freedom. The reality was rather different. It was neatly summarised in a sharply-worded *Independent* editorial dating from 23 May 1988: 'we now live in a society whose representative figure is the moneyed yob'.

In the specific area of education policy, contradictions and uncertainties have been numerous. Thatcher's intellectual advisers were clearly divided over something as fundamental as the desirability or otherwise of a national curriculum. Was it really compatible with either devolution of power to individual schools, or true market principles? Then again, if there was, in fact, 'no such thing as society' (as Margaret Thatcher proudly announced in an interview published in *Woman's Own* in October 1987), what was to be the basis of teaching about the social order?

Among a number of questions associated with the school curriculum were the following: How were primary schools to be expected to cope with a subject-based curriculum designed primarily for the secondary sector? Was TVEI to be welcomed as a liberating curriculum initiative? Or should it – as the Right insisted – be retained solely for the 'less able' and the 'non-academic'? Was there still a role for vocational and practical courses in the upper secondary school, or would all the subjects specified in the 1988 Act leave no time for their pursuit? Perhaps most important of all, how would any form of voucher system work, once supposedly popular schools reached the point where they were no longer able to accommodate all the pupils seeking admission?

The 1988 Act introduced many changes to the education system of England and Wales. In many ways, however, it generated more questions than answers.

NOTES

1. Quoted in P Wilby and S Midgley, 'As the New Right Wields Its Power', *Independent*, 23 July 1987, p.11.
2. See Griggs, op cit.
3. Reported in Wilby and Midgley, op cit.
4. Hillgate Group, *Whose Schools? A Radical Manifesto* (Hillgate Group, London, 1986).
5. S Sexton, *Our Schools: A Radical Policy* (Institute of Economic Affairs, London, 1987), p.10.
6. See, in particular, A Gamble, *The Free Economy and the Strong State: The Politics of Thatcherism* (Macmillan, London, 1988).
7. R Scruton, *The Meaning of Conservatism* (Macmillan, London, 1980).
8. See P Cordingley and P Wilby, *Opting Out of Mr Baker's Proposals* (Education Reform Group, London, 1987).
9. Quoted in the *Independent*, 7 June 1988.
10. Reported in the *Independent*, 13 November 1987.
11. Department of Education and Science, *The National Curriculum 5-16: A Consultation Document* (DES, London, 1987).
12. *Hansard*, H of C, vol 123, col 771, 1 December 1987.
13. See D Lawton, *The Politics of the School Curriculum* (Routledge and Kegan Paul, London, 1980).

14. Interview on Local Education Authorities Project (LEAP) video, *Accountability*.

15. See, for example, B Simon, '10/65 and All That', *Times Educational Supplement*, 13 July 1990.

16. Hillgate Group, op cit, p.18.

17. B Simon, *Bending the Rules: The Baker 'Reform' of Education* (Lawrence and Wishart, London, 1988).

18. J Thomas, 'Pupils as Vouchers', *Times Educational Supplement*, 2 December 1988.

19. P. Brown, 'Education', in P. Brown and R. Sparks (eds), *Beyond Thatcherism: Social Policy, Politics and Society* (Open University Press, Milton Keynes, 1989), 33-47, pp.40-1.

5 EDUCATION REFORM: REVERSALS AND AMENDMENTS

Implementation of the many measures contained in the Education Reform Act 1988 did not go entirely smoothly. The government found itself forced to alter aspects of its policy as new objections or obstacles arose. Particular problems were encountered in the twin areas of curriculum and assessment policy.

ORIGINS OF THE NATIONAL CURRICULUM

A number of commentators locate the origins of the Conservatives' national curriculum in the Ruskin College speech delivered by Labour premier James Callaghan in 1976. In this speech, 'the strong case for the so-called "core curriculum" of basic knowledge' was listed as one of the subjects that 'need study because they cause concern'. Similarly, in a confidential DES memorandum of the same year (usually known as the Yellow Book), it was argued that 'the time has probably come to try to establish generally accepted principles for the composition of the secondary curriculum for all pupils'.[1]

Picking up on these themes, an editorial in the *Times Educational Supplement* of 17 April 1987 argued that the events of 1976 'clearly laid the groundwork for most of the centralising initiatives of the next decade'. The *Guardian's* education correspondent, Maureen O'Connor also claimed that the Ruskin speech marked a watershed in educational thinking, stating that,

> In 1976 Prime Minister James Callaghan shattered the complacency of parts of the educational establishment by launching a major political attack on Britain's schools... In the succeeding ten years, following the Great Debate of 1976/77, a curriculum consensus has emerged which has survived changes of government and Secretaries of State.[2]

In a 1987 booklet designed to accompany a television series on education, former *Times Educational Supplement* editor Stuart Maclure argued similarly that the new national curriculum should be viewed primarily as the culmination of a centralising process which began in 1976:

> The Callaghan Speech and the Great Debate which followed…
> changed the relationship between the DES and the education sys-
> tem. The long-term trend towards central control was strengthened.
> The taboo on government intervention in the curriculum was broken.
> It would be another ten years before ministers would talk quite
> openly of their desire for a national curriculum; but the process of
> achieving one began at Ruskin.[3]

The argument made by each of these commentators is, however,
unconvincing and misleading. It is certainly true (and has already
been argued here) that the Callaghan government created a broad
educational consensus which lasted for at least a decade. This was
built around moves towards more central control of the curriculum
and subordination of the secondary curriculum to perceived 'needs'
of the economy. It is also true that the idea of a national curriculum has
its origins in curriculum debates of the late 1970s.

Yet the notion of a bland continuity of approach embracing all players in
the drama cannot be sustained. Civil servants in the DES did argue
consistently for more central control of the curriculum as an effective
means of increasing teacher accountability. They received some support
from HMI, which favoured a common curriculum for all schools which
was far more developed than the DES idea of a limited core of subjects
imposed from the centre.[4] Bureaucrats did, then, maintain a consisten-
cy of approach during the 1970s and 1980s.

Politicians, by contrast, did not. Sir Keith Joseph may have upset his right-
wing supporters by working broadly within the educational consensus
created by the last Labour administration. Yet even he did not
embrace the concept of centralised curriculum control, finding that
this did not fit with his neo-liberal leanings. In consequence, as late as
March 1985 the second Thatcher government issued a key White
Paper which included the following statement:

> it would not in the view of the Government be right for the
> Secretaries of State's policy for the range and pattern of the five to sixteen
> curriculum to amount to the determination of national syllabuses for that
> period. It would, however, be appropriate for the curricular policy of the
> LEA, on the basis of broadly agreed principles about range and pattern,
> to be more precise about, for example, the balance between curricular
> elements and the age and pace at which pupils are introduced to par-
> ticular subject areas (e.g. a foreign language)… The Government does not
> propose to introduce legislation affecting the powers of the
> Secretaries of State in relation to the curriculum.[5]

Furthermore, as has already been argued, the desirability or otherwise of curriculum uniformity was the key issue which divided right-wing pressure groups as they drew up plans for the 1988 Act. For the IEA and CPS, arguments in favour of curriculum control represented the last gasp of a dying consensus. Only members of the Hillgate Group actually wanted a national curriculum, and they saw it largely as a tool of social control. Without their support, and the persistence of a significant section within the DES, the national curriculum would never have found its way into the 1988 Act. Its very existence has been a source of embarrassment for the Right ever since. Indeed, half-hearted support for the national curriculum among those who originally drafted the 1988 Act helps to account for both its hasty preparation, and treatment it subsequently received at the hands of respected curriculum planners.

POLICY MAKING AND THE NATIONAL CURRICULUM

It can hardly be disputed that the original national curriculum consultation document, issued in 1987, was greeted with a chorus of disapproval on the part of a large body of teachers and educationists. The government being understandably reluctant to give publicity to the views of its critics, it was left to Julian Haviland, former political editor of the *Times*, to publish (at the beginning of 1988) a book, *Take Care, Mr. Baker!*, analysing the 20 000 or so replies received by the DES to the spate of discussion documents issued while the Educational Reform Bill was in preparation.

Of these, over half (11 790) concentrated on the national curriculum. So hostile were they that the government was obliged to give a misleading impression of their overall flavour. Minister of State Angela Rumbold told a supporter on 19 January 1988 that of all the representations, only 1536 were opposed to the idea of a national curriculum. As Haviland points out, her answer was accurate. It was also, however, incomplete. The principle of a national curriculum was overwhelmingly approved in the replies received by the DES. Yet not one response endorsed without reservation the actual curriculum structure proposed by the government.

It was certainly felt by many that plans for the 1988 Act in general, and for the national curriculum in particular, had been prepared with too much secrecy and without the benefit of widespread consultation. In the words of Peter Cornall, Senior County Inspector for Cornwall, speaking in September 1987,

Many of us have no quarrel with a largely common curriculum: on the contrary, we have been trying for years to convert others by example. What we could not have foreseen is the manner in which all this is happening, a manner so ill-matched to an issue of such fundamental national importance. Surely the foundations of no lasting monument are laid in obscurity, by artificers whose credentials cannot be scrutinised? A forum much nearer in character to a Royal Commission, consisting of known persons, presenting a Report beyond all suspicion of partisan influence or short-term considerations, could have commanded support and good-will, far beyond what even the most thorough and competent of Civil Service papers can expect to do. Instead, we have the gravely-flawed product of amateurs, a hasty, shallow, simplistic sketch of a curriculum, reductionist in one direction, marginalising in another, paying only a dismissive lip-service to the professional enterprise and initiative on which all progress depends.[6]

The manner in which the national curriculum was introduced was, then, a clear indication that the 'partnership years' in education were truly over. It appeared to suggest, moreover, that HMI, local advisers and teachers themselves were all to be excluded from the policy-making process. Speaking in January 1988 (following introduction of the Education Reform Bill into the House of Commons the previous November), former HMI Chief Inspector Sheila Browne reflected on some of the changes that had taken place since her own departure from the Inspectorate in 1983:

Apart from the Government's growing impatience with the slowness of developments, what has changed most is the sad decline of working trust between and among the partners in education and, at times, the substitution of a mode of public confrontation which seems sometimes so blind that it is ready to deny the self-evident right, if it emanates from any source except itself.[7]

Browne went on to suggest that the government's attitude had to change, for the sake of education itself.

CRITICISM OF THE CONTENT OF THE NATIONAL CURRICULUM

The national curriculum consultation document was also criticised by a number of teachers and lecturers for its narrow, subject-based instrumental approach. Lawton argued in the *Times Educational Supplement* of 18 September 1987 that,

There is nothing wrong with subjects, provided they are treated as *means* and not as *ends*. Virtually all the enlightened views on curriculum planning are now agreed that subjects should be regarded as important only if they help to reach other objectives which, in turn, have to be justified… All this is ignored in the Government's consultation document: no justification is put forward for the selection of the foundation subjects; no argument put forward to give priority to the core subjects; no attempt made to relate subjects to wider objectives.

Similarly, the notion of ten foundation subjects was characterised as both 'vague and mechanistic' in a letter sent to the *Independent* by a group of academics at the University of Sussex, which was published on 14 October 1987:

The subjects listed seem to be no more than lumps extracted from the curriculum *status quo* which the Government happens to approve of. What we need… is some appreciation of the broad unifying categories (humanities, arts, sciences), which, when placed properly together, might come to represent some kind of balance.

As far as the primary sector was concerned, the government's simplistic framework was interpreted by many as a cynical rejection of that primary-school approach to curriculum planning which refused to endorse the secondary school's obsession with subject boundaries. In a speech delivered to the *Forum* conference 'Unite for Education' held in London in March 1988, Michael Armstrong, head of a primary school in Oxfordshire, argued that primary teachers' philosophical objection to a subject-based curriculum was not simply a matter of the need to find room for the ubiquitous primary school 'topic':

It is rather that most of the really fruitful classroom inquiries, whether on the part of an individual child, a small group of children, or an entire class, have a way of moving in and out of subjects, conflating traditions, confusing boundaries, eliminating distinctions and creating new ones. So a study of the life of a frog becomes an exercise in philosophical speculation, scientific observation, literary fantasy and artistic method. So designing a set of earrings turns into an investigation of the psychology of faces. So an examination of mathematical powers embraces the geography of the universe and the mythical origins of the game of chess… In learning… all the significant insights tend to come to those, teachers and pupils alike, who refuse to be bounded by subjects, who are prepared to move freely *between* traditions and *beyond* traditions – from science to philosophy to art to some new field of inquiry – without embarrassment. For every significant curriculum rewrites to some degree the history of knowledge.[8]

FURTHER CRITIQUES

Other commentators identified other problems. Among them were the very real difficulty of fitting recent curriculum initiatives in the area of technical and vocational studies into the new highly-congested timetable for the last two years of secondary schooling. Also criticised was the government's perceived neglect of the issue of children with special educational needs. Similarly, its failure to make space for local initiatives in the area of multicultural/anti-racist education was challenged.[9]

Many of these criticisms were reiterated and expanded in a book of essays on the national curriculum published by the University of London Institute of Education in 1988. It was emphasised that the new proposals were chiefly concerned with controlling what was taught in schools and making teachers generally more accountable for their work in the classroom.[10] In the area of special educational needs, the Education Bill was seen to take no account of those 18 per cent of children with special needs being taught in ordinary schools without Statements.[11] It was also argued that the national curriculum and its related testing programme could well have the effect of labelling children 'failures' at an early stage of their primary schooling and stifling innovation and initiative in the primary-school classroom.[12]

Beyond these criticisms, it was pointed out that the government's curriculum could hardly be described as 'national' since its provisions did not extend to pupils in independent schools. Indeed, this distinction prompted a number of awkward questions:

> What concept of a national curriculum and of a national education – indeed what concept of a nation – underlies this decision? Is it that teachers in independent schools can be trusted to provide a balanced curriculum and appropriate standards of education whilst the teachers in state schools cannot? Is it that pupils in independent schools can be trusted to make the right choice of subjects and to work hard, whilst those in state schools cannot? Could it be an attempt to hold down standards in independent schools? Or is the purpose of this... proposed legislation to promote a widening of those curricular and broader educational differences which have been such a recurring feature of the education system in this country since the nineteenth century?[13]

BAKER'S RESPONSE

Education Secretary Kenneth Baker took the unusual step of referring to this Institute of Education publication in an address to the North of England Education Conference in January 1989:

> During the public debate on education both before and after the 1987 general election some remarkably censorious things were said – seldom by me. Teaching staff of the London Institute of Education, for example, said that the Government's National Curriculum framework had so little to commend it that it brought into disrepute the very concept of a common curriculum for the nation's schools. The National Curriculum was described as 'a folly of unprecedented proportions'. And another contributor said that it was hard to see all this resting intact 'under the critical barrage which it has already undergone and may be expected to suffer in the next few months'.

Baker conceded that a speech outlining his plans for a national curriculum delivered at the North of England Education Conference in 1987 had met with a frosty reception. He nevertheless went on to argue that the mood among educationists had profoundly changed in the intervening two years:

> Successive reports on aspects of the National Curriculum have appeared and been recognised as solid pieces of professional work. Professor Paul Black's report on tests and assessments [the TGAT Report]; the reports on English by Sir John Kingman and Professor Brian Cox; Mr Graham's report on mathematics; Professor Thompson's report on science; and Lady Parkes' report on technology – each in turn has elicited respectful comment and triggered off constructive debate. The *Guardian* – not always enthusiastic about the Government's education policies – has written of the Cox Report on English: 'the ship is moving in the right direction. Ministers have every right to feel satisfied about a difficult job well done'. The *Economist* has recently said that 'instead of Britain looking abroad to find cures for our ills, other countries are now looking at us to see how they can emulate our success'. The Professor of Education at Cambridge [David Hargreave] has recently said that my policies are not radical enough.[14]

BATTLE OVER THE WHOLE CURRICULUM

There was some justification for the Education Secretary's somewhat complacent observations. Various working party reports, especially the

Task Group on Assessment and Testing (TGAT) Report, and statutory orders (outlining what has to be taught in schools) reassured teachers (if only temporarily) that the government's right-wing advisers would not have things all their own way. Furthermore, the new National Curriculum Council under the leadership of Duncan Graham appeared to be prepared to stand firm against political pressure to impose a narrow grammar-school curriculum.

In 1990 the NCC won the battle over whether or not the national curriculum could really be thought of as 'the whole curriculum'. The *Times Educational Supplement* of 3 January 1992 reported that Graham himself had described this victory as 'the National Curriculum Council's finest hour'. The seminal NCC document, *Curriculum Guidance 3: The Whole Curriculum*, published in March 1990, argued that the national curriculum alone could not provide the broad and balanced curriculum to which all pupils were entitled. It identified five themes which, although by no means constituting a comprehensive list, appeared to be essential ingredients of a successful curriculum, particularly at the secondary stage:

- Economic and industrial understanding
- Careers education and guidance
- Health education
- Education for citizenship
- Environmental education

These themes could be either separately timetabled or subsumed within existing areas of the curriculum. At the same time, among other provisions in the document, the NCC insisted that certain non-statutory dimensions must underpin all teaching in schools: notably, a commitment to providing equal opportunities for all pupils, and a recognition that preparation for life in a multi-cultural society was relevant to all pupils.

IMPLEMENTATION FAILURE

On the negative side, there is one very important area where the national curriculum has proved to be incapable of implementation. The story of Key Stage Four is undeniably one of amendment, confusion and eventual abandonment.[15] It is also a useful reminder that policy formulation and policy implementation do not necessarily amount to the same thing.

Within two years of passage of the 1988 Act, it became obvious to government that Key Stage Four simply could not survive in the form originally envisaged by the DES. To begin with, there were severe practical problems involved in fitting so many separate subjects (along with a number of cross-curricular themes) into a finite amount of curriculum time. On top of this, many teachers complained that it would be extremely difficult to teach all ten core and foundation subjects (as well as religious education) to pupils of all abilities without incurring pupil resentment and opposition. Furthermore, as the general economic situation worsened and young people experienced increasing difficulty in finding work, there seemed to be a renewed need for the sort of vocational and technical courses that had been popular in the first half of the 1980s.

Speaking in January 1990, Education Secretary John MacGregor announced that he was reviewing the requirement that schools should teach 14-16 year-olds all national curriculum subjects for a reasonable time. He revealed that he had asked vocational examination bodies such as the Business and Technician Education Council and the Royal Society of Arts to submit qualifications for approval, as part of a new policy of providing 'a wider range of options' for older students.[16]

In another speech at the end of July 1990, the Education Secretary signalled a further strategic retreat on national curriculum arrangements for Key Stage Four by suggesting that some pupils might be allowed to 'drop' certain subjects from the age of 14. Most likely to be 'dropped' were art, music and physical education. However, the position of history and geography was also put in doubt. MacGregor made it clear that the national curriculum would remain intact up to the age of 14, but that, for the next two years, pupils might well be obliged to take only five of the ten foundation subjects. These would be the three core subjects of English, maths and science, plus technology and a foreign language. The Education Secretary was prepared to concede in this speech that Key Stage Four posed its own special problems. 'Essentially, the question is one of fit – how to achieve a broad balanced curriculum for all pupils without sacrificing worthwhile options... There is a genuine dilemma here.'[17]

Interviewed by the *Daily Telegraph* on 30 October 1990, Education Minister Tim Eggar announced that the government had decided to encourage secondary schools to develop a vocational alternative to the academic curriculum. In his view,

> Far too many children from 14 upwards are studying things which they and their teachers do not regard as appropriate... We have to offer these youngsters the sort of vocational courses and qualifications that will make sense to them – and encourage them to stay on in full-time education after the age of 16.

Schools would now be encouraged to develop parallel 'academic' and 'vocational' streams, with the main objective being to enhance the status of vocational qualifications:

> That is the main issue facing us in education. That is the area where we are so much weaker than Germany – not in turning out graduates, but in producing skilled workers and supervisors... To achieve that, we must now have two parallel streams – the vocational and the academic – from half-way through secondary school, so that children can concentrate on what interests them.

Finally, Education Secretary Kenneth Clarke effectively abandoned Key Stage Four of the government's national curriculum in January 1991. Ignoring NCC advice that all ten national curriculum subjects should remain compulsory to the age of 16, he announced that he had finally decided that only science, maths and English should remain 'sacrosanct' in the last two years of schooling. Pupils would now be able to 'drop' art, music and history or geography, with physical education being treated 'flexibly'. All pupils would still have to study a modern language and technology, but would not be compelled to take GCSEs in them.

The new arrangements were defended as a means of ensuring that, once again, schools could cater for pupils according to their differing job prospects. In Clarke's words,

> I believe we should not impose on young people a rigid curriculum that leaves little scope for real choice. By the age of 14, young people are beginning to look at what lies beyond compulsory schooling, whether in work or further study. We must harness that sense of anticipation if every pupil is to have the chance of developing to the full.[18]

THE THREE WISE MEN

At the same time, the Education Secretary was also planning to impose his views concerning teaching methods and classroom organisation on Britain's primary-school teachers. Throughout 1991, Clarke made it clear that he wanted to see a return to so-called traditional methods whereby pupils are 'streamed' from an early age and then taken through a programme of study in specific subjects. Interviewed by the *Times* on 4 November 1991, he asserted that,

> What has been regarded as good practice in primary schools in recent years can't deliver because it is too play-centred, too child-centred... There is a great deal of this play-centred teaching... which means at its weakest, there is a lot of the sticking together of egg boxes and playing in sand.

At the beginning of December 1991, Clarke commissioned an inquiry into primary-school teaching methods, indicating that a report would be produced by the end of January 1992. The time of year, together with the choice of three men as 'experts', led the media to dub the investigators the 'Three Wise Men'. They were asked to review available evidence about the delivery of education in primary schools and to make recommendations about curriculum organisation, teaching methods and classroom practice appropriate for the successful delivery of the national curriculum, particularly at Key Stage Two.

In launching the investigation, Clarke indicated that he expected the resultant report to attack child-centred teaching methods and to recommend a return to whole-class teaching. It was already clear that the whole debate about learning was to be simplified so that it could be polarised for popular consumption.

When the report was published, it was immediately hailed by Clarke as a vindication of his earlier criticisms of primary-school methods. In actual fact, it refused to endorse one single method of grouping children and rejected the idea of class streaming. It also declined to outlaw topic work in schools and recommended that there should be 'a mix of good subject teaching and topic teaching'. One of the report's authors, Professor Robin Alexander of Leeds University, later complained in the *Independent on Sunday* of 2 February 1992 that the Education Secretary had 'hijacked' and 'misinterpreted' the report for political purposes.

ASSESSMENT POLICY: TGAT

The principle of a national curriculum was finally accepted, albeit reluctantly, by many of the government's right-wing advisers on the grounds that it would justify a major programme of pupil testing at certain key stages. Comparison of results could then be used to reveal the strength of some schools and expose the shortcomings of others.

It is certainly clear that from the very beginning, Prime Minister Margaret Thatcher and Education Secretary Kenneth Baker clashed over the nature and status of external testing in the national curriculum. Thatcher wanted externally set tests. Baker, by contrast, accepted the need for an element of school-based assessment. The eventual compromise involved institution in July 1987 of the Task Group on Assessment and Testing under the leadership of Professor Paul Black. This was given the very difficult challenge of devising a workable scheme of assessment within six months.

TGAT's first report was produced on 24 December 1987 and published in January 1988. Three supplementary reports followed at the end of March 1988. A digest of the first report was also produced for discussion in schools. The proposals contained in these reports were far more sophisticated than anything envisaged by either the Prime Minister and her allies or the educational world in general.

The approach adopted by Black's team built on assessment procedures and practices already in existence, improving on them where appropriate, and relating them to specific problems posed by the national curriculum. One general assumption made by TGAT was that, far from distracting classroom teachers from the teaching-learning process, good assessment would actually help teachers, particularly in primary schools, to know more about their pupils. It would therefore enable them to teach more effectively.

The two major surprises in the TGAT proposals were Standard Assessment Tasks (SATs), and a system of 'levels of attainment'. The 'tasks' were meant to be sufficiently wide-ranging to avoid curricular distortion. The levels were designed to allow for differentiation, variation and progression. One very important aspect of the proposed structure was its rejection of the concept of simple, externally-assessed 'pass/fail' tests, though it was accepted that publication of school performance would be an integral part of the new system.

COMPROMISE SOLUTIONS

The TGAT recommendations were essentially an uneasy compromise. They appeared to find a role for professional expertise, while simultaneously giving civil servants and politicians the kind of information they needed for purposes of accountability, control and the efficient running of a market system of schools. Pupil scores could be aggregated to show results for a class, a school and even a whole LEA for comparative purposes. This was, however, precisely the sort of information parents could use to make superficial judgments about the desirability or otherwise of individual schools.

It was nevertheless a compromise which failed to satisfy right-wing think-tanks. In March 1988, the CPS published a short pamphlet, *Correct Core: Simple Curricula for English, Maths and Science*, which rejected complex assessment procedures and contained simple examples of what around 85 per cent of pupils could be expected to do by the ages of 7, 11, 14 and 16. Moreover, Thatcher was persuaded by her right-wing friends that Baker had allowed the government's assessment plans to be 'hi-jacked' by detested 'professionals'.

A letter sent from the Prime Minister's Office to Kenneth Baker's Private Secretary (and printed by the *Independent* on 10 March 1988) indicates the extent to which Thatcher was dissatisfied with the main proposals in the TGAT Report. The leaked letter, reproduced below, describes at some length the Prime Minister's chief reservations:

From Paul Gray (Prime Minister's Private Secretary)
To Tom Baker (Secretary of State for Education's Private Secretary)

21st January 1988

Dear Tom,

re: National Curriculum Task Group on Assessment and Testing Report

The Prime Minister has had the opportunity to look in more detail at this Report which your Secretary of State published last week. Although she agreed to your Secretary of State welcoming the Report as the broad framework into which attainment targets could be fitted, there are a number of aspects which she finds disturbing.

First, the Committee seem to have designed an enormously elaborate and complex system. They suggest it requires setting up two new powerful bodies: the Schools and Examinations Council and the National Curriculum Council, and a major new role for the LEAs. Is this necessary? And has the sort of approach advocated in the Report in fact been put into practice with the proposed degree of elaboration in any large group of schools?

Second, the Prime Minister notes that the philosophy underlying the Report is that tests are only a part of assessment, and that the major purpose of assessment is diagnostic and formative, rather than summative. As a result, the method of assessment places a heavy responsibility on teachers' judgements and general impressions. She is also concerned to note the major role envisaged for the LEAs in the implementation of the whole system.

Third, the Report does not pull together the overall costs of the exercise, but the general impression is that these would be very large ... the Prime Minister wonders whether, for example, the Group has considered the likely costs of training teachers prior to implementation and the regular annual costs of teachers' time once the system is in operation.

Fourth, the Prime Minister also notes that, presumably as a result of the complexity of the proposals, the new assessment system could not be introduced in less than five years. Although she recognises the importance of the careful preparation and introduction of the new arrangements, she is concerned that the process might take too long.

The Prime Minister would be grateful if your Secretary of State could take these concerns into account in his further considerations of the Report and the continuing dialogue with the Task Group.

Yours,

Paul Gray

ABANDONMENT OF TGAT'S PROPOSALS

The story of assessment since 1988 has been one of gradual abandonment of the Task Group's complex proposals. Classroom teachers themselves gave Thatcher a belated victory of sorts. Indeed, it could be argued that the Right's obsession with standardised, pencil-and-paper, 'objective' tests has now triumphed, largely because it has proved almost impossible for teachers to implement the Task Group's complicated structure.

It was realised even at the pilot stage in 1990 that whatever their merits in terms of a diagnostic view of assessment, the TGAT proposals were costly, cumbersome and time-consuming. For example, maths, science and English involved a total of 32 'attainment targets' for Key Stage One alone. There were to be 227 'statements of attainment' for maths, science and English, which meant that for a class of thirty 7 year-olds, a teacher would need to grapple with as many as 6810 'statements of attainment'.

By the end of 1990, the government was having to modify its original demands, deciding, for example, that tests at the end of Key Stage One should cover only nine 'attainment targets' instead of the original 32. Even so, the SAT procedures of 1991 proved to be deeply controversial. Not only were problems of teacher workload and disruption to useful education caused by testing highlighted. It was also found by teachers that SATs largely confirmed their previous estimates of individual abilities and gave no opportunity to explore children's potential.

The testing of 7 year-olds has steadily become more straightforward since 1990. There is moreover a certain irony in the fact that at its conference in Bournemouth at the end of May 1992, the National Association of Head Teachers (NAHT) passed a motion stating that the government's tests were now 'too simplistic to yield useful information about children's progress'.[19]

1992 has also seen the introduction of pencil-and-paper tests for 14 year-olds. Four out of five pupils in both state and private schools sat six one-hour tests in maths and science over a period of two days as part of a pilot testing programme. English and technology will be added when the tests are extended to 14 year-olds in all state schools in 1993.

Finally, the government in summer 1992 announced plans to test 11 year-olds (at the end of Key Stage Two) from 1994. Tests will be formal and written, and will last a total of four and a half hours. They will be in English, maths and science, and will be undertaken during one week in May. They will obviously have selection as well as assessment implications, and will be introduced in 1994.

NOTES

1. See Chitty, op cit, pp.89,94,116-7.

2. M O'Connor, 'Ruskin Ten Years On', *Contributions* 11 (Centre for the Study of Comprehensive Schools, York, 1987), 2-10, p.2.

3. S Maclure, *Promises and Piecrust* (Community Unit, TVS, Southampton, 1987).

4. In a number of key texts, HMI argued for the school curriculum to be constructed in terms of a number of 'areas of experience' and rejected the DES concept of a subject-based core curriculum.

5. Department of Education and Science, *The Curriculum from 5 to 16* (HMSO, London, 1985).

6. Quoted in M O'Connor, *Curriculum at the Crossroads* (School Curriculum Development Committee, London, 1987).

7. Reported in the *Times Educational Supplement*, 8 January 1988.

8. M Armstrong, 'Popular Education and the National Curriculum', *Forum* 32 (1990), 68-73.

9. On this last point, see in particular W Ball and B Troyna, 'The Dawn of a New ERA? The Education Reform Act, "Race" and LEAs', *Educational Management and Administration* 17 (1989), 23-31.

10. C Chitty, 'Two Models of a National Curriculum: Origins and Interpretation', in D Lawton and C Chitty (eds), *The National Curriculum* (Institute of Education, University of London, 1988), 34-48.

11. The 1978 Warnock Report estimated that around 20 per cent of children might at some time in their schooling have 'special educational needs'. In accordance with the provisions of the Education Act 1981, LEAs are required to maintain a 'Statement' in the case of those children whose 'needs' are such as to necessitate special educational provision. The picture varies from one part of the country to another. However, approximately 2 per cent of children are in special schools or similar provision. This roughly corresponds to the percentage of pupils with Statements. It is therefore evident that the majority of pupils with special educational needs are in ordinary schools. The only reference to special educational needs in the original Education Bill of 1987 occurred in Clause 10, which permitted the national curriculum to be modified in the case of those children with Statements. Mary Warnock now appears to believe that the 1981 Act has not really worked.

12. C Gipps, 'What Exams Would Mean for Primary Education', in Lawton and Chitty, op cit, 65-77.

13. R Aldrich, 'The National Curriculum: An Historical Perspective', in Lawton and Chitty, op cit, 21-33.

14. Department of Education and Science, 'Vote of Confidence for National Curriculum', press release 3/89, 6 January 1989.

15. See C Chitty, 'Key Stage Four: The National Curriculum Abandoned?', *Forum* 34 (1992), 38-40.

16. Reported in the *Times Educational Supplement*, 2 February 1990.

17. Reported in the *Guardian*, 1 August 1990.

18. Reported in the *Guardian*, 5 January 1991.

19. Reported in the *Guardian*, 28 May 1992.

6 THE POLITICS OF CHOICE

In recent years, the politics of choice have been a central theme of Conservative rhetoric in the educational sphere (as in many others). Conservative practice has, however, failed in many respects to live up to the rhetoric of choice. The real extent of choice in British education, and alterations to that extent, during the period of Conservative rule in the 1980s and 1990s therefore require investigation.

HISTORY OF THE POLITICS OF CHOICE

Restorationists in Conservative ranks tend to see the educational future in terms of an idealised past. They seek a return to the golden age of the 1950s and early 1960s when, it is claimed, a tripartite system ensured that there was genuine parental choice of secondary schools.

Yet in reality no such choice ever existed. Those children who failed the eleven-plus selection examination and who did not have parents wealthy enough to afford independent school fees were virtually forced to attend one of the local secondary moderns. The tripartite system was, in fact, a crude bipartite system. As late as 1958 – 14 years after passage of the Butler Act – less than 4 per cent of the secondary cohort had access to a genuine secondary technical school.

When comprehensive reorganisation began to develop substantially in the 1960s, the question of defining suitable catchment areas for the new schools posed very real problems for LEAs experimenting with reform. In predominantly rural ares, it was comparatively easy to allocate a certain number of towns and villages to each school. In large urban areas, where schools were in easy travelling distance of one another, the situation was fraught with difficulties.

The Inner London Education Authority experimented with the idea of dividing all its 11 year-olds into seven ability bands, the distribution being based on results of primary school tests. In this way it sought to ensure that all comprehensives, at least in theory, taught children of all abilities. Other LEAs favoured the concept of 'neighbourhood' or 'community' schools, accepting that this might well lead to some comprehensives having single-class intakes. Others saw future success in terms of creating for each school a 'social mix', anticipating a steady amelioration of social-class differences through pupils' experience of working together in a common secondary school.

Labour Education Secretary Shirley Williams (1976-79) had marked reservations about universal application of the comprehensive ideal and was anxious to see choice and diversity in education utilised as vote-winning issues for the Labour government.[1] She even toyed with the idea that each LEA should create a number of 'super comprehensives'. These would specialise in particular subjects and would thereby be able to attract pupils on the basis of their distinctive curricular expertise. In this respect, Williams was very much ahead of her time, anticipating by some 15 years one of the key initiatives more recently associated with the London Borough of Wandsworth under Donald Naismith and with John Major's new Education Secretary John Patten.

Yet it would be wrong to see educational ideas discussed during the three years of Callaghan government as having the truly radical overtones of measures currently favoured by the Right. Williams had no plans to allow market forces to dictate the future shape of schooling. She accepted the general principle of a state education system, locally administered. She even came to realise that her plans for guaranteeing parental choice of schools were both unworkable and elitist.

It was Energy Secretary Tony Benn who played the leading role at Cabinet level in defeating the Education Secretary's attempt to introduce a new Education Act focused on the issue of secondary-school choice. Once Williams' consultative document on the subject became available for general discussion among leading members of the party, he was able to argue, both at a Cabinet meeting in October 1977 and in a subsequent letter to the Prime Minister, that the vast majority of LEAs, of whatever political persuasion, were already taking parental choice into account and operating successful admissions and appeals procedures. To guarantee all parents a place for each of their children at the secondary school of their choice was simply to create expectations that no government or LEA could possibly meet.

Moreover, the continued existence of grammar schools in many areas made it impossible to legislate for parental choice of secondary school without, at the same time, giving harmful legislative recognition to eleven-plus selection:

> While grammar schools still remain in being, as they do, any parental choice set out as an objective in legislation must also provide that that choice cannot be exercised into a grammar school by children who do not have the requisite ability... Since therefore the consultative document suggests that parental choice has to be limited by 'the age, ability and aptitude of the pupils', the proposed Bill could actually appear to be, and the Courts might make it become, a route back to the legalisation of selective secondary education, at a time when our real task is to complete the comprehensive development in the secondary sector.[2]

Williams was forced to take note of the opposition aroused by her proposals, and to concede that it would be almost impossible for the DES to draft a Bill which would be legally watertight.

Education Secretary Sir Keith Joseph (1981-86) was also committed to the concepts of choice and diversity, and he certainly had very little respect for the comprehensive principle. Yet he failed to secure reintroduction of selection in Solihull and elsewhere, and so began to devote his energies to creating different educational routes within the comprehensive school. Interviewed on *Weekend World* in February 1984, he emphasised the importance of differentiation as a guiding educational principle: 'If it be so, as it is, that selection between schools is largely out, then I emphasise that there must be differentiation within schools'.

Interestingly, the Solihull debacle provided the Conservative Party with convincing evidence that while grammar schools might still be popular with many middle-class parents, there could be no going back to the days of a universal competitive examination at eleven-plus. As Walford and Jones show, it was a well-organised group of middle-class parents which effectively sabotaged the ill-judged attempt to claim Solihull as a 'victory' for the grammar-school lobby.[3] These parents were largely resident in affluent areas in the south of the borough, and their children were already well served by local comprehensive schools with good academic reputations and very active parent-teacher associations. To turn one or more of these comprehensives into grammar schools, with ability as the sole criterion for entry, could only have the disastrous effect of allowing the middle-class monopoly of places at these schools to be challenged by able Birmingham overspill children living in the north of the borough. The plan was duly defeated.

CITY TECHNOLOGY COLLEGES: PLANNED DEVELOPMENT

The Education Reform Act 1988 can be viewed, at least in part, as an attempt to create new types of secondary school with selective implications without, at the same time, subjecting children to the strain of a competitive examination at eleven. In other words, it seeks choice and diversity without overt selection.

Taking first the plan for a network of city technology colleges, it becomes apparent that this constitutes an interesting link between the agenda of so-called 'Conservative Modernisers', which seeks to increase the prominence of technology in the school curriculum, and that of New Right think-tanks, which seeks to undermine the power of LEAs.

Official announcement of the CTC plan was made by Kenneth Baker in a speech to the 1986 Conservative Party conference. From the start, it was stressed that CTCs would be both independent of LEA control, and partly funded by the private sector. The colleges would be expected to develop enterprise, self-reliance and responsibility, and would enhance parental choice of secondary schools. There would be no written entry examination, but selection procedures would clearly have to operate. These would lay particular stress on the 'attitudes' of applicants and their parents. Evidence of a commitment to making the most of a technology-orientated curriculum would be very important.

Further details of the new concept were published in *A New Choice of School: City Technology Colleges*, the promotional brochure published by the DES in October 1986:

> Their purpose will be to provide a broadly-based secondary education with a strong technological element, thereby offering a wider choice of secondary school to parents in certain cities and a surer preparation for adult and working life to their children.[4]

It was clearly stated that CTCs would be new schools for 11-18 year-olds. They would be established in urban areas alongside existing secondary schools. Each CTC would be registered as an independent school and would therefore be free from LEA control. None would charge fees. The catchment area served by each CTC would be substantial, and the composition of its intake would be broadly representative of the local community. Individual sponsors would meet all or a substantial part of initial capital costs, with the Secretary of State being responsible for running costs. The curriculum would be broad and balanced, but would include a large technical and practical element.

The 1986 brochure made it clear that the government was prepared to fund up to 20 CTCs in the initial phase of development. It identified 27 possible locations, including Hackney and Notting Hill in London, the St Paul's area of Bristol, Handsworth in Birmingham, Chapeltown in Leeds, Knowsley on Merseyside and the Highfields district of Leicester. A number of the areas listed suffered acute social deprivation and were already receiving priority attention through the Inner City Initiative.

THE REALITY OF CITY TECHNOLOGY COLLEGE DEVELOPMENT

Six years on, even a number of Conservatives have been forced to admit that the CTC plan has been a costly failure.[5] Indeed, it can be argued that the original concept has been changed dramatically in the light of severe setbacks. This has been particularly true in the case of both funding and provision of suitable sites.

Of 1800 major firms initially approached for help with financial contributions, fewer than 20 responded positively. This has resulted in the Exchequer having to bear most of the capital and running costs of the new schools. In the case of Djanogly CTC in Nottingham, for example, which eventually opened in autumn 1989, the government agreed at an early stage in negotiations to sanction a £9.05 million Treasury contribution to augment the £1.4 million which had been subscribed by public companies. This prompted the *Times Educational Supplement* to comment with uncharacteristic bitterness on 27 May 1988:

> Just what sort of a public education initiative is it which puts up over £9 million from public funds for one 'private' school? And just what sort of priorities are being pursued when one, as yet unbuilt, private school gets £9.05 million, while the county of Nottinghamshire's entire capital allocation is less than £2.5 million?

On the day in September 1990 on which John MacGregor opened the £9 million CTC in Bradford, Shadow Education Secretary Jack Straw took television cameras to two state schools in other parts of Bradford. One was composed entirely of Portakabins and had an open walkway between classrooms. The other had sewage from the lavatories seeping into the playground. It was pointed out that both could have been replaced at a quarter of the cost of the CTC. According to the Education, Science and Arts Select Committee, capital expenditure on all CTCs in 1990-91 was estimated to be £49.01 million, of which only £5.07 million came from private sources.

The CTC plan has also been undermined by the government's failure to find suitable sites for the new schools. Interviewed in the *Times Educational Supplement* of 17 June 1988, Kenneth Baker's special CTC adviser Cyril Taylor admitted that the government had been far too optimistic in 1986. Costs of refurbishing and equipping redundant schools and green-field sites had, he said, been 'woefully underestimated by the Department of Education and Science'. The new aim was to buy up schools already in use and 'phase in' CTCs over a period of up to six years. Taylor claimed that this would help the government to 'rescue its project', while at the same time 'broadening' the CTC concept:

> We are approaching councils like Croydon, Bexley and Kent and asking them to sell us the most deprived or failing school ... Instead of creating a new school which then threatens others, we will try to make the existing school better ... The CTCs are no longer a pilot scheme. I predict that eventually one in four secondary schools will become CTCs.

In actual fact, a total of 15 CTCs will be in existence by autumn 1993.

GRANT-MAINTAINED SCHOOLS: POLICY CHANGE AND DEVELOPMENT

From the government's point of view, the proposal to allow schools to opt out of LEA control has also so far met with a disappointing response. In July 1992, grant-maintained status had been accorded to 287 establishments in England and Wales out of a total of 25 000 state schools (of which almost 21 000 are primary and 4200 are secondary). This amounted to just 1.2 per cent of eligible schools.

From the outset, the proposal itself was shrouded in considerable confusion. It has since been subjected to frequent amendment. In May 1987 education junior minister Bob Dunn proudly announced to a meeting of Conservative supporters that new government proposals to allow schools to take as many pupils as they could physically manage, in tandem with plans to give heads control of school budgets and the right to opt out of council control, were all parts of a grand strategy that would eventually lead to 'the denationalisation of education'.[6] Similarly, at a pre-election press conference in the same month, Margaret Thatcher argued that heads and governors who opted out of local authority control should be free to establish their own admissions policies, and would not necessarily be prevented from raising extra funds through parents (thereby prompting media speculation that the new plans might include a fee-paying element).[7]

Indeed, when interviewed on *World at One* on 10 June 1987, Kenneth Baker conceded that there was nothing in the new plans to stop 'better-off parents' raising additional resources for an opted-out school. These resources might be used by the headteacher to purchase particularly expensive books and items of equipment, and perhaps even to pay teachers higher salaries. Later DES statements, however, were anxious to play down the fee-paying aspect, and even to deny that the opt out policy was really a covert means of reintroducing secondary selection.

Confusion reigned throughout the autumn of 1987, when Baker made a determined effort to preserve a certain degree of independence for the DES machine. Interviewed on 14 September 1987 in the *Independent*, Thatcher looked forward to a situation where 'most secondary schools' would choose to opt out of the locally administered state system. Baker, by contrast, predicted on *Panorama* on 2 November 1987 that only a minority of schools would choose to do so. Similarly, Thatcher hoped that popular comprehensive schools which opted out of the system would soon elect to change their character and become selective, whereas Baker expected most comprehensives to choose to remain comprehensive.[8]

Maclure has argued that 'no provisions in the 1988 Act aroused stronger feelings than those on grant-maintained schools'.[9] In fact, this was one area where the government was forced to take note of its critics as the 1987 Bill was subjected to 370 hours of often heated debate during its passage through parliament. The House of Lords voted by a majority of 19 to insist that the opting-out process be backed by a majority of parents eligible to vote, rather than simply by a majority of those voting This was later modified by the government when the Bill returned to the Commons. In the final version of the 1988 Act, the result of a ballot on opting out is determined by a simple majority of those voting, provided only that 50 per cent of registered parents have taken part. If less than 50 per cent take part, a second ballot must be held within 14 days of announcement of the result of the first. The outcome of this second ballot is conclusive, irrespective of turn-out.

ADVANTAGES OF GRANT-MAINTAINED STATUS

Why, then, might a school find it desirable to seek grant-maintained status? Several reasons may be cited. The school might be a comprehensive seeking to become selective, though this has rarely proved to be the case. The government initially stated (though this provision did not appear in the Act itself) that a school could apply for a change of status only after five years had elapsed, such that a time-lag would in any case exist.

The school might be a grammar school finding itself 'threatened' by comprehensive reorganisation. Alternatively, it might be a comprehensive school facing closure or the loss of its sixth form as a result of new LEA plans for post-16 provision. In fact, the first two schools to be accorded grant-maintained status (in February 1989) were Skegness Grammar School in Lincolnshire and Audenshaw High School in Tameside, Greater Manchester. Tameside Council, which had wanted to close Audenshaw High, was forced to abandon its reorganisation plans, stating that there was no longer any point in putting any school up for closure.[10]

The most compelling reason for a school to opt out is probably financial. The original DES circular on grant-maintained schools, published in October 1988, stated unequivocally that, 'grant-maintained schools will compete *on equal terms* with LEA-maintained schools, and will be funded *on the same basis* as other schools in their neighbourhood'.[11] This has certainly not been the case. Indeed, implementation of opting out has so far cost the DES over £30 million in additional expenditure.[12]

After a series of denials, John Major himself finally forced admitted, in August 1991, that opted-out schools were being given special financial treatment in an attempt to encourage more to take up the option. In a letter to the General Secretary of the National Union of Teachers (NUT) he wrote:

> We have actually made no secret of the fact that grant-maintained schools get preferential treatment in allocating grants to capital expenditure. We look favourably at grant-maintained schools to

encourage the growth of the sector, and I am delighted to see that numbers are continuing to grow rapidly.[13]

Disillusioned by the slow rate of take-up, the government has tried by various means to make opting out a more viable and attractive option. John MacGregor told the 1990 Conservative Party conference that all primary schools, regardless of size, would now be eligible for grant-maintained status. Headteachers were urged to resist the 'bully-boy tactics' allegedly being adopted by both Conservative and Labour councils to keep schools under their control. On 25 April 1991, Kenneth Clarke formally announced the abandonment of the five-year restriction on grant-maintained schools changing their character.

FUTURE PROSPECTS FOR GRANT-MAINTAINED SCHOOLS

Despite this feverish activity, many on the right of the Conservative Party remained far from satisfied with the general rate of progress under both Margaret Thatcher and John Major. By 1992, many of their number felt that, after thirteen years of Conservative rule, remarkably little had been done to embrace the concept of unbridled parental choice. They looked forward to a time when, following a Conservative victory in the 1992 general election, most schools, and especially secondary schools, would be encouraged to opt out of the control of despised LEAs and become grant-maintained.

Such a development would both destroy the power of LEAs and contribute to the diversity of schools in the maintained sector. With strategic planning by LEAs a thing of the past, the notion of a local 'system' of schools would be steadily replaced by that of a network of separate, semi-autonomous, competitive institutions maintained to a limited extent by central government. This, then, was the prospect offered by a fourth term of Conservative rule.

NOTES

1. See Chitty, *Towards a New Education System*, pp.156-8.
2. Letter from Tony Benn to James Callaghan, 26 October 1977, Benn archive.
3. G Walford and S Jones, 'The Solihull Adventure: An Attempt to Re-Introduce Selective Schooling', *Journal of Education Policy* 1 (1986), 239-53.
4. Department of Education and Science, *A New Choice of School: City Technology Colleges* (HMSO, London, 1986), p.2.
5. When the initial project was announced it apparently 'chilled the blood' of Philip

Merridale, leader of the Conservative group on the Council of Local Education Authorities, and later a founder member of the moderate Conservative Education Association.

6. Reported in the *Times Educational Supplement*, 15 May 1987.

7. Reported in the *Guardian*, 23 May 1987.

8. Reported in the *Observer*, 30 September 1987.

9. Maclure, op cit, p.56.

10. Reported in the *Guardian*, 23 February 1989.

11. Department of Education and Science, *Education Reform Act: Grant-Maintained Schools*, Circular 10/88 (DES, London, 1988).

12. Local Schools Information, *Opting Out 1988-1992: An Analysis* (LSI, London, 1992).

13. Reported in the *Guardian*, 7 August 1991.

7 EDUCATION AFTER THE AGE OF SIXTEEN

Of particular interest to a number of writers about education are the kinds of provision which should be made for people above the school leaving age of 16. Educational provision for post-16s has for many years been inadequate in Britain. In the 1980s debate of this issue ran parallel to wider debates about educational reform.

AN EARLY SELECTION, LOW PARTICIPATION SYSTEM

The 1960s and early 1970s were years of enormous expansion in 16-19 education and training in many leading industrial nations, a large number of which were determined to compete with the technological advances so heralded in the Soviet Union.

In the United Kingdom, however, rates of participation did not expand at a comparable rate. Even as late as 1981, only 18 per cent of 16-18 year-olds were in school in Britain. In Japan the figure was 58 per cent. In the United States it was as high as 65 per cent. Selected figures for participation in full-time education and training of 16-18 year-olds in all types of institution – not just schools – in 1981 demonstrate that the picture here is equally gloomy for Britain. These figures are reproduced in Table 7.1.

Table 7.1 Participation in full-time education and training of 16-18 year-olds in seven countries, 1981

	%
United States	79
Netherlands	71
Japan	69
France	58
Italy	47
Germany	45
United Kingdom	32

Source: Department of Education and Science, *Statistical Bulletin 10/85* (HMSO, London, 1985).

By the end of the 1980s, the situation appeared to be changing quite dramatically. A survey carried out by careers officers and published in April 1991 found that the proportion of 16 year-olds in England and Wales continuing in full-time education had risen from 48 per cent in 1989 to 53 per cent in 1990. Staying-on rates were above the national average in London, the South East, the South West and Wales. They were below average in the Midlands and the North.

These findings came just days after an attack by Prince Charles on Britain's educational standards, in which he stated that their most alarming feature was the small proportion of young people between 16 and 18 in full-time education. They were seized upon by Education Secretary Kenneth Clarke as a means of arguing that the reality about staying-on rates was 'very different from the gloomy pictures we keep hearing about'.[1]

The trend towards continuing in full-time education beyond the statutory period appeared to be confirmed by the next set of figures released by the careers service, in June 1992. These showed that the proportion of young people staying on at school or college had risen by a further eight percentage points in 1991 to a new high of 61 per cent. What was not clear was whether this was the result of recession, which made it very difficult for 16 year-olds to find work, or of a new-found interest in the pursuit of qualifications for their own sake.

An optimistic view about the increasing appeal of post-16 courses is not one that all would share. Indeed, on close examination the careers service figures, while welcome, mask a reality which actually provides very little cheer. As Ken Spours and Michael Young pointed out in a letter published in the *Guardian* on 7 May 1991, the rise in full-time staying-on rates reflects a more contradictory situation than that outlined in many newspaper reports.

Recent studies in inner-city areas have shown that while staying on is still very much influenced by the decline in the labour market, it is also fuelled by under-achievement at school. Many 16 year-olds in effect repeat their fifth year and leave at the age of 17. There is very little evidence that the range of post-16 opportunities is proving a decisive influence, as many like to claim. Indeed, it is quite clear that many 16 year-olds are on inappropriate courses, in particular those simply leading to GCSE re-sits. A detectable rise in student aspirations is not being matched by widespread introduction of relevant and innovative courses which would encourage more sustained staying on.

What is, in fact, being witnessed is a rise in short-term participation which points to the inadequacy of our current qualifications system. Recent DES statistics show that the proportion of 16-18 year olds in full-time education and training in Britain is still very low compared with the figures for our major economic competitors. These statistics are reproduced in Table 7.2.

Table 7.2 Participation in full-time education and training of 16-18 year-olds in five countries, 1986-88

	%
United States (1986)	79
Japan (1988)	77
France (1986)	66
West Germany (1987)	47
United Kingdom (1988)	35

Source: Department of Education and Science, *Statistical Bulletin* (HMSO, London, 1990).

Spours and Young concluded their 1991 *Guardian* letter with the observation, 'The real issue is to make sure our qualification system is reformed to ensure that more young people can achieve substantially higher levels of qualification at 18, giving access to higher education and higher-skilled jobs'.

Clearly Britain's failure to cater for youngsters' needs at the post-16 stage has seriously affected the proportion of teenagers moving on to some form of higher education. According to the Vice Chancellor of Salford University, John Ashworth, speaking in 1987, 'We are brilliant at educating a small, highly academic elite, but very poor at educating the majority of the population'.[2]

At the beginning of 1988, Green was able to claim that Britain has 'the highest rate of early school leaving, the lowest rate of achievement in nationally recognised qualifications, and the lowest rate of participation in higher education of almost any country in Europe, except Portugal and Spain'. At the end of the 1980s, Britain had around 15 per cent of the relevant age group in higher education, compared with 20 per cent in Germany who were at university or polytechnic, 30 per cent in the United States who went on to study at degree level, and 37 per cent in Japan who went on to college or university.[3]

ALTERNATIVE STRATEGIES FOR THE FUTURE

What, then, needs to be done about Britain's early selection, low participation system? Can our qualification system be transformed to ensure the creation of a more highly-skilled workforce and the widening of access to all forms of higher education?

In July 1990, the Institute for Public Policy Research (IPPR) published *A British Baccalaureat* as its first Education and Training Paper.[4] Its sub-title – 'Ending the division between education and training' – succinctly defines the IPPR's distinctive approach.

The paper criticises A-level courses for being over-specialised, old-fashioned and elitist. It condemns vocational training for being too narrow and job-specific and for not aiming high enough. It accuses employers in the labour market of encouraging early entry to work through inflated youth wages, age limits on entry into training schemes and poor recompense for those with qualifications.

Far from seeking to reform the present divided system, it argues that only abolition of the separation of academic from vocational studies can serve as the starting-point for change. It therefore proposes a new unified system of education and training leading to a single Advanced Diploma, the British bac of the title. The system would be designed to encourage substantially greater full-time participation post-16, but would also guarantee education-led opportunities for those who did not choose to stay on full-time. In contrast to the present qualifications system, which has all the features of an educational obstacle course, the new arrangements would amount to a late selection, high participation system appropriate to the needs of the twenty-first century.

At the institutional level, the IPPR report recommends a system of tertiary colleges as the most effective and efficient means of delivering unitary, education-led post-16 provision. Since, however, it would not be feasible to legislate for an immediate switch to tertiary college-based education post-16, the report proposes that in some areas the existing mixed economy of institutions should persist. However, to generate positive change even in the short term it suggests that that mixed economy should develop into a series of 'tertiary systems' through increased collaboration and the sharing of common curricula and qualifications.

THE GOVERNMENT'S RESPONSE

None of this has found favour with the present government, which outlined a totally different approach to the problem of post-16 provision in the White Paper *Education and Training for the 21st Century*, published in May 1991. This describes how sixth form and further education colleges are to be severed from LEA control and financed by new funding councils. It argues for development of new diplomas recording achievement in academic and vocational qualifications. It declares that schools will be allowed to admit part-time and adult students to their sixth forms. Crucially, it refuses to contemplate reform of A-levels, and comes down firmly in support of a divided system, albeit with marginally greater flexibility for transfer and combination within different areas.

Whereas the IPPR envisages a unitary, education-led post-16 system, the government simply wants to remove existing barriers to equal status between 'the so-called academic and vocational routes'. Henceforth, academic and vocational qualifications are to be held in equal esteem. Yet it is not at all clear how this is to be made to happen, particularly when ministers continue to refer to the A-level as the 'gold standard'.

ACCESS TO HIGHER EDUCATION

Where, finally, does all this leave the problem of access to higher education? In a speech at Lancaster University in January 1989, Education Secretary Kenneth Baker called for a doubling (to around 30 per cent) of the proportion of young people going into universities or polytechnics over the next 25 years. However, he made it clear that the expansion he anticipated in higher education should be based on American models of private funding, rather than on the West European system of increased public finance. Subsequently, his immediate successor John MacGregor, in an interview with the *Guardian* on 24 November 1989, abandoned the target of 30 per cent, adding that he was still committed to some expansion of student numbers, but 'only on a realistic and affordable basis, with funding coming from a variety of sources'.

By the time the White Paper, *Higher Education: A New Framework*, was published in May 1991, one in five of all 18-19 year-olds was entering higher education each year, compared with around one in seven only four years earlier. The White Paper anticipates that approaching one in three of all 18-19 year-olds will be moving on to higher education by the year 2000. The key to expansion is said to lie in greater competition for funds and students, which, it is argued, can best be achieved by ending the artificial distinction between universities and polytechnics. However, the White Paper refuses to commit itself to a major increase in public expenditure, maintaining that 'it is in the interests of universities, polytechnics and colleges to continue to look for increased levels of funding from private sources'. The need to contain public spending clearly means that emphasis will continue to be placed on 'cost-effective expansion'.[5]

In these circumstances, the chances of wider access to a high-quality university education seem remote. The issue of education after the age of 16 is likely to remain contentious during the 1990s.

NOTES

1. Reported in the *Guardian*, 26 April 1991.
2. Quoted in O'Connor, 'Ruskin Ten Years On', p.2.
3. A Green, 'Lessons in Standards', *Marxism Today*, January 1988, 24-30.
4. The IPPR was created in 1988 by leading figures in the academic, business and trade union worlds to counterbalance the very great influence of right-wing think tanks.
5. Department of Education and Science, *Higher Education: A New Framework*, Cmnd 1541 (HMSO, London, 1991).

8 EDUCATION IN THE EARLY 1990s

The Education Reform Act 1988 did nothing to re-establish consensus in education. On the contrary, it served if anything to polarise debate yet further. Education in the early 1990s was a very contentious issue.

EDUCATION AT THE START OF THE 1990s

By the end of the 1980s, roughly 7 per cent of secondary pupils in Britain were being educated in independent schools. There were, of course, regional variations. In particular, south east England registered a higher than average proportion of independent schooling. Within the publicly-provided system of education, more than 90 per cent of the relevant age group were attending comprehensive schools in England. The figure was yet higher in Wales, and reached nearly 100 per cent in Scotland. These data are reproduced in Table 8.1.

Table 8.1: Number and percentage of pupils in comprehensive secondary schools in Great Britain, by country, 1965-66 to 1986-87

	England		Wales		Scotland	
	Pupils	%	Pupils	%	Pupils	%
1965-66	26	9.9	50	28.3	–	–
1970-71	1072	36.3	112	58.5	184	58.7
1975-76	2777	74.8	208	88.5	349	87.6
1980-81	3436	89.5	231	96.6	392	96.0
1982-83	3392	90.6	230	97.4	385	96.5
1983-84	3339	91.3	227	98.0	377	96.7
1984-85	3221	91.3	223	98.4	363	96.4
1985-86	3118	92.0	215	98.5	361	100.0
1986-87	2991	92.3	207	98.5	344	100.0

Note:
1. Numbers are expressed in thousands.
2. Totals for England from 1970-71 include a component to account for middle-school pupils deemed to be of secondary school age
Sources: *Education Statistics for the United Kingdom*, 1986 and 1988.

In the summer of 1992, there were still 156 grammar schools in England and Wales, concentrated in 28 LEAs. As can be seen from

Table 8.2, within the maintained sector the proportion of English pupils in grammar schools stabilised at just over 3 per cent in the 1980s. This figure may, of course, rise dramatically if a significant number of grant-maintained schools choose to apply for selective status.

Table 8.2: Pupils in different types of maintained secondary schools in England, 1978-87

	Pupils '000	Middle %	Comp-ive %	Modern %	Grammar %	Tech %
1978	3851	6.7	76.1	10.0	5.1	1.5
1979	3872	6.9	79.1	8.5	4.2	1.4
1980	3866	6.9	81.4	6.8	3.7	1.2
1981	3840	7.0	82.5	6.0	3.4	1.1
1982	3780	7.1	82.9	5.6	3.3	1.1
1983	3741	7.0	83.6	5.1	3.1	1.1
1984	3646	6.9	84.4	4.7	3.2	0.8
1985	3526	6.8	84.5	4.7	3.2	0.7
1986	3389	6.6	85.4	4.2	3.0	0.7
1987	3240	6.5	85.8	4.1	3.1	0.5

Source: Department of Education and Science, *Statistical Bulletin* 6/88, (DES, London, 1988).

Despite the government's open hostility towards, and disparaging remarks about, the comprehensive system, it is clear that secondary reorganisation has meant very real benefits for the children of this country. Using examination results as a very narrow (though nonetheless important) criterion of success, the DES White Paper *Better Schools*, published in March 1985, reported that one in five students was now gaining at least one A-level pass, compared with only one in seven during the 1960s. In addition, more than a quarter of pupils (27 per cent) were now obtaining five O-level 'pass' equivalents, against only a fifth 20 or so years earlier.

From substantial research on the effects of comprehensive reorganisation in Scotland, McPherson and Willms concluded at the end of the 1980s that,

> Since the mid-1970s, the reorganisation that was initiated in 1965 has contributed both to a rise in examination attainment and to a fall in the effect on attainment of social class. We call these two trends respectively 'improvement' and 'equalisation'.[1]

A meticulous review of the impact of comprehensive reorganisation in Britain led Glennerster and Low to conclude in 1990 that:

> The main and really major improvements in exam performance were achieved by the average-ability students, and they were achieved mostly in the comprehensive schools... It is a tribute to the state schools that they produced both more qualified leavers and the structural changes politicians were demanding.[2]

As was noted in Chapter Seven, Britain has no cause to feel complacent about its education system, particularly when its achievements are measured against those of our European competitors. At the very basic level of public expenditure on education, the UK lags well behind many European countries, as can be seen from Table 8.3.

Table 8.3: Public spending on education as a percentage of gross domestic product in 23 countries, 1986-87 and 1987-88

	1987-88	1986-87
Denmark	7.50	7.17
Sweden	7.19	7.49
Netherlands	6.99	6.55
Norway	6.82	6.56
Canada	6.53	6.64
Austria	5.91	6.03
Ireland	5.84	5.89
France	5.57	5.59
New Zealand	5.37	4.93
Finland	5.31	5.23
Australia	5.25	5.27
Belgium	5.12	5.42
Switzerland	5.01	5.10
Japan	4.98	5.10
United Kingdom	4.97	5.04
Italy	4.96	–
United States	4.77	5.03
Portugal	4.26	4.10
Germany	4.24	4.31
Luxembourg	4.09	–
Yugoslavia	3.55	3.55
Greece	2.70	2.88
Turkey	1.59	2.03

Source: Chartered Institute of Public Finance and Accountancy.

However, it is at least clear that the standard of British education would be much worse had the divided system of the 1940s and 1950s been maintained.

THE CONSERVATIVES' POSITION

Yet this evidence is ignored by the present government. The 1988 Act, and the 1992 White Paper can be viewed as representing both an attack on locally-organised systems of comprehensive schooling and a belief that what it provides is essentially second-rate education.

John Major's own hostility towards comprehensive schooling was made clear in a four-page letter to Fred Jarvis, former general secretary of the NUT, which was released to the press at the end of February 1992. In this remarkably frank letter, which was more outspoken than any pro-nouncement of Education Secretary Kenneth Clarke, the Prime Minister seemed anxious to blame comprehensive schools for all the fail-ures of the education system. His blanket condemnation accused the Labour Party of having introduced a system which fostered low standards and expectations:

> I am drawn to the view that the problem of low standards stems in large part from the nature of the comprehensive system which the Labour Party ushered in in the 1960s, and from the intellectual climate underpinning it that has tended to stress equality of outcome at the expense of equality of opportunity.

> The orthodoxy which has grown up around the comprehensive system has, frankly, been an orthodoxy of the Left: hostility to competition *between* schools and *between* pupils, and even in sport; hostility to test-ing; hostility to genuine parental choice; and a steady infiltration of traditional curriculum subjects such as history and English Literature by some questionable dogmas that fly in the face of common sense.

> I ask you not to doubt my sincerity and determination to reverse the fail-ings of the comprehensive system and the cycle of low expectations and low standards which it has fostered.[3]

Indeed, the government was anxious to make clear before the 1992 elec-tion that opted-out schools could become grammar schools without difficulty. As early as February 1991, Kenneth Clarke said he was not unduly worried if his critics saw the opt out policy as 'a back-door attempt to re-introduce grammar schools'. Alternatively, he would be happy if grant-maintained schools decided to become 'magnet schools'. In other words, pupils would be admitted on the basis of their aptitude for specific subjects such as science, technology or art and design.[4]

Clarke reiterated these views, particularly for the benefit of those who might think Thatcherism had been abandoned, when interviewed by Jonathan Dimbleby for the BBC1 television programme *On the Record* broadcast on 21 April 1991. As has already been noted in Chapter Six, only four days later, he formally lifted the restriction on grant-maintained schools which prevented them from 'changing their character' within five years of opting out of LEA control.

The Education Secretary again used the BBC's *On the Record* programme at the beginning of February 1992 to emphasise to Tory 'hardliners' that the Government would like to see the return of grammar schools as part of a more diverse state education system. On this occasion he sprung what the *Times* called 'a pre-election surprise' by indicating that he would have 'no problem with one grant-maintained school in ten becoming a new grammar school'. He made it clear that grammar schools could reappear throughout the country, 'as long as there were not too many in each area'. The government, he said, was simply anxious to respond to local pressures:

> We have no objection to the re-emergence of grammar schools, if that is what the parents want... Parents will decide; schools will decide ... I am simply responding to their demands as they set out the separate characteristics they want to adopt... The stigma attached to secondary modern schools will be avoided through the growth of magnet schools: technological schools and others with different specialisms... We have got to get away from the idea that the only good education is, in fact, an academic education, and that the only good qualification is an academic one.[5]

Anxious to dispel the notion that Margaret Thatcher's departure marked a change in the direction of educational policy making, the first Major government was also ruthless in bringing both the NCC and the SEAC – the two main bodies specifically established by the Education Reform Act 1988 to oversee curriculum and assessment procedures – under direct government control. In mid-July 1991, the chairs (and chief executives) of both these bodies suddenly 'retired'. First to go was Duncan Graham of the NCC. He was followed a week later by Philip Halsey of SEAC. Both were replaced (in their chairing roles) by political nominees: Graham by David Pascall, former member of the Downing Street Policy Unit (DSPU) and senior BP manager; Halsey by Brian Griffiths (now Lord Griffiths of Fforestfach), formerly head of the DSPU and subsequently chair of the CPS.

In an editorial on 21 July 1991, the *Independent on Sunday* commented, 'When the history of twentieth-century British education is written, the past ten days will be seen as a watershed. The Government has dropped any pretence that the National School Curriculum should be ideologically neutral'. Thatcher would probably have described Pascall and Griffiths as 'two of us'; but it is debatable whether she would have dared to make such appointments when the 1988 Act was first implemented.

THATCHERISM AND MAJORISM

Part of the reason for the Conservatives' (unexpected) success in the 1992 general election lies in the fact that they were able to convince a large part of the British electorate that there had already, in a sense, been a change of government. This had come in November 1990, when John Major replaced Margaret Thatcher.

It was useful for some Conservatives to be able to argue that removal of Thatcher from Downing Street had ushered in a gentler, more compassionate form of Conservatism. Others preferred to see Majorism, if such a philosophy actually exists, as simply the continuation of Thatcherism by other means: a marked change of style perhaps, but not of content. Others again expected that the fall of Thatcher would necessitate a brief period of marking time, to be followed by full-blooded resumption of Thatcherite policy after a fourth convincing Conservative election victory.

Indeed, this was the fervent hope expressed in a lengthy *Times* editorial published on 11 April 1992, two days after the general election. It also argued in passing that Thatcher herself had waited too long before embarking on the most important stage of her ambitious social project:

> Mr Major has been a good Prime Minister. He is now a national leader who has risen to the challenge of combat to beat a strong opponent. He deserves his party's plaudits… The plainest advice to him now, from all who encouraged him to victory, is that he should now

press on with the mission begun by his predecessor, Margaret Thatcher, back in 1979. That mission, left virtually in abeyance since 1990, was to dismantle the corporate state, whose aggrandisement has dominated postwar politics not just in Britain but across Europe. The task is attitudinal as much as practical. It was made harder by Mrs Thatcher's slowness in implementing her plans... Mr Major may have to face another election before his full term is up. The team he puts together... should be a team suited to fighting again alongside him on the hustings. His Queen's Speech must possess more 'radicalism' than he has yet shown. He should make it a new 'Hundred Days' programme of Tory reform.

The former Prime Minister herself was in no doubt that Major would be forced to continue her work since, as she argued in her famous post-election *Newsweek* article of 27 April 1992, there is, in fact, no such thing as Majorism:

> I don't accept the idea that, all of a sudden, Major is his own man. He has been Prime Minister for 17 months, and he inherited all those great achievements of the past $11^1/_2$ years which have fundamentally changed Britain, ridding it of the debilitating, negative aspect of Socialism...

> There isn't such a thing as Majorism. There couldn't be, at the moment. My colleagues and I turned round the whole philosophy of government. We restored the strength and reputation of Britain. We did it on fundamental principles. They bear my name, but they are far older than I am. Mr Major has accepted these principles, written them into his manifesto, held it up and said: 'It's all me'. What he means is that the things put in there were *his* choice. But I believe he will be forced to take *my* legacy forward...

> Thatcherism will live. It will live long after Thatcher has died, because we had the courage to restore the great principles and put them into practice, in keeping with the character of the people and the place of this country in the world.

It has already been argued that in the field of education policy the former Prime Minister has no real need to worry about her successor's loyalty to Thatcherism. Major's philosophy can be described as an interesting mixture of concern for Thatcherite privatising measures and a more traditional Conservative belief in the values of a meritocratic society. He is thus a creature both of the Old Right and the New. In his ideal world, schools will increasingly compete for pupils by offering specialisations, with parents using league tables as guides to LEA (while such bodies still exist), school and pupil performance. HMI will be privatised and schools will become increasingly accountable to non-professional opinion.

Throughout the 1992 general election campaign Major stressed that he wanted to see all schools free from council control, rewarding 'good' teachers and open to choice by parents. In the view of Stephen Bates, education correspondent of the *Guardian*, education is increasingly coming under Major's personal direction: 'There is no doubt he's got his dander up. Every announcement bears the stamp of a hankering after what appears to be the very sort of 1950s grammar-school education that let him down so badly'.[6]

THE EDUCATION AGENDA IN 1992

By the time John Patten was appointed Education Secretary following the 1992 general election it was clear that a number of educational issues still required urgent attention. On the one hand, the Education Reform Act 1988 was failing to meet the objectives of its New Right initiators. On the other, provisions within the Act itself were causing all manner of unforeseen administrative difficulties.

The CTC project was drawing to a depressing close, with only 15 colleges in existence or certain to open. Some New Right pressure groups may be concerned about the vocational emphasis of the CTC curriculum, but at least the new colleges are independent of LEA control. At the same time, there were fewer than 300 grant-maintained schools in existence, and the government had actually turned down the only application from such a school to become selective (in this case, a middle school where selective procedures would not be easy to operate). Moreover, there was considerable evidence that opting out was not taking off all over the country but was, in fact, popular in authorities that were either Conservative or low-spending (or both).

According to a comprehensive analysis carried out by Local Schools Information and published in February 1992, schools wanting to opt out of local council control had so far been concentrated in only 12 of the 117 education authorities in England and Wales. The advice organisation analysed the 428 decisive opt-out ballots that had been held since implementation of the Education Reform Act in July 1988. Of these, voters in 97 schools had been opposed to opting out, with 331 in favour. Of these 331 'favourable' results, 187 had been approved by the

Secretary of State (166 secondary schools and 21 primaries); 32 had been rejected; and 112 were still at that time awaiting a final decision.

Of the 204 English secondary schools voting to opt out and not affected by reorganisation plans, 103 were in the 25 lowest spending LEAs (48 in Kent and Lincolnshire alone), and only 12 were in the 25 highest spending. In 36 councils (31 per cent of the total) no opt-out ballots had been held. More than half the ballots, 219 (or 51 per cent) had been held in only 12 of the 117 LEAs (Bromley, Dorset, Ealing, Essex, Gloucestershire, Hertfordshire, Hillingdon, Kent, Lincolnshire, Norfolk, Northamptonshire and Surrey). Opt-out applications had, in fact, snowballed in a number of Conservative authorities: 47 ballots had been held in Kent, 25 in Lincolnshire, 24 in Essex, 19 in Norfolk, and 18 in Surrey. In total, 13.2 per cent of secondary schools in Conservative-controlled LEAs had voted to opt out, compared with only 2.2 per cent in Labour LEAs. A hugely disproportionate number of opt-out ballots had been held by grammar schools: of the 156 grammar schools in England and Wales, 57 (37 per cent) had held opt-out ballots.[7]

Administratively, the co-existence of grant-maintained and LEA secondary schools makes local planning almost impossible, and has generated chaos in schools' admissions systems in certain areas. This was particularly the case in summer 1992. Parents are currently able to make multiple applications, often trying for a place at an opted-out, grant-maintained school, a CTC (where such an option exists) and an LEA school. When the LEA school makes an offer, parents often hold it until they have heard from the grant-maintained school or the CTC. This effectively ties up a place and prevents the LEA from offering it to someone else. A further complication is a recent high court ruling that LEAs cannot give priority to their own residents over those from neighbouring authorities. Some would like to see a university-style clearing system set up for admission to secondary schools. However, the government has so far failed to act on this suggestion.

SELECTION AND SPECIALISATION

Research carried out by a team at the University of Leicester and published in 1992 reveals that a third of the first comprehensive schools to opt out have used some form of selection when over-subscribed.[8] Still, however, the government's erstwhile supporters have been dismayed by a number of aspects of the opt-out project: its potential for administrative confusion;

its failure to secure converts, particularly in those Labour areas where it was thought schools would queue to escape LEA control; and, above all, its failure (so far at least) to be the means by which the country could return to the divided system of the 1950s.

In consequence, the government has experimented with new ideas for reintroducing secondary selection without returning to the days of the dreaded secondary modern school. The new 'in-word' to replace selection appears to be specialisation. Britain is now to have a version of American 'magnet schools': in other words, selection by specialisation. The government has learned the lesson of the Solihull debacle of the 1980s and will not risk incurring the wrath of middle-class parents by bringing back eleven-plus selection. Instead, a new strategy is being pursued. Details of the new 'schools revolution' were enthusiatically reported as the front-page story in the *Mail on Sunday* of 3 May 1992:

> Education Secretary John Patten is looking at plans to turn secondary schools into centres of excellence in key subject areas... This means that some schools will specialise in academic subjects like languages, maths and science; some will be technically-based; and others might offer performing arts or sport as their new specialism... The move puts selection back on the education agenda – but it drives a final nail in the coffin of the campaign to bring back grammar schools and the 11-plus.

The Education Secretary himself argued in an article in *New Statesman and Society* published on 17 July 1992 (shortly before the appearance of his White Paper), that socialists must now come to terms with specialisation:

> ... selection is not, and should not be, a great issue of the 1990s as it was in the 1960s. The S-word for Socialists to come to terms with is, rather 'Specialisation'. The fact is that children excel at different things; it is foolish to ignore it, and some schools may wish specifically to cater for these differences. Specialisation, underpinned by the National Curriculum, will be the answer for some – though not all – children, driven by aptitude and interest, as much as by ability...

> It is clear that on to the foundation-stone of the National Curriculum can be built the liberation of all the talents through greater specialisation in our schools. This could be specialisation *within* a large comprehensive setting for this or that subject – by their pupils self-selecting, or being guided towards it by aptitude and commitment. Or it could be something that builds on to the schools – a leading edge in bilingually-taught technology, for example, or in music, or where languages crucially meet business studies...

Such schools are already emerging. They will, as much more than mere exotic educational boutiques, increasingly populate the educational landscape of Britain at the end of the century, a century that introduced universal education at its outset; then tried to grade children like vegetables; then tried to treat them... like identical vegetables; and which never ever gave them the equality of intellectual nourishment that is now offered by the National Curriculum, encouraged by testing, audited by regular inspection.

On this basis were developed the government's new education proposals, which seek to complete the work begun in 1988.

NOTES

1. A McPherson and J D Willms, 'Comprehensive Schooling is Better and Fairer', *Forum* 30 (1988), 39-41.
2. H Glennerster and W Low, 'Education and the Welfare State: Does It Add Up?', in J Hills (ed), *The State of Welfare: The Welfare State in Britain since 1974* (Clarendon Press, Oxford, 1990), 28-87.
3. Reported in the *Guardian*, 28 February 1992.
4. Reported in the *Times Educational Supplement*, 1 March 1991.
5. Reported in the *Times*, 3 February 1992.
6. The *Guardian*, 7 July 1992.
7. Local Schools Information, op cit.
8. Reported in the *Observer*, 12 April 1992; and in the *Times Educational Supplement*, 3 July 1992.

9 THE 1992 WHITE PAPER AND BEYOND

At least in the educational sphere, the Major administration set itself the task of completing the series of radical reforms on which its predecessor administration had embarked. Majorism was to be the culmination of Thatcherism. At the centre of its educational thinking was John Patten's White Paper of July 1992.

THE 1992 WHITE PAPER

The 1992 White Paper *Choice and Diversity: A New Framework for Schools* was published on 28 July 1992, to form the basis for new legislation in autumn 1992. Launching the 64-page document, much of which he wrote himself, Patten described it as 'a blueprint for the state system for the next 25 years'. He went on: 'Our proposals are radical, sensible and in line with what parents want... This is above all a common sense White Paper. Its central focus is on choice and diversity.[1]

In the foreword to the White Paper, John Major wrote,

> Our reforms rest on common sense principles – more parental choice; rigorous testing and external inspection of standards in schools; transfer of responsibility to individual schools and their governors; and, above all, an insistence that every pupil everywhere has the same opportunities through a good common grounding in key subjects. Few people would now argue with these principles. They are all helping to shape a more open, a more responsive and a more demanding system of education... I am not prepared to see children in some parts of this country having to settle for a second-class education. Education can make or mar each child's prospects. Each has but one chance in life.[2]

The White Paper argues that five important themes run through the history of educational change in England and Wales since 1979: quality, diversity, increasing parental choice, greater autonomy for schools and greater accountability. The proposals contained in the White Paper are claimed explicitly to complete the process begun by Margaret Thatcher's government in 1979:

The five themes have provided the framework for the Government's aims, and together define our goal for Britain's education system. The measures necessary to achieve that goal are now largely in place. This White Paper and the proposed legislation that flows from it will complete the process.[3]

PROPOSALS IN THE WHITE PAPER

The White Paper makes a number of key proposals:

- The opting-out process will be 'streamlined' and speeded up, with limits placed on LEA spending on 'counter-propaganda'. It is anticipated that, on a simple projection of current trends, there could be over 1500 grant-maintained schools in existence by April 1994, and more than 4000 a year later. By 1996, most of the country's secondary schools, as well as a significant proportion of the maintained primary schools, could be grant-maintained. Henceforth, primary schools will be able to opt out in 'clusters'.

- The DFE will hand over responsibility for channelling funds to grant-maintained schools to a new statutory body, the Funding Agency for Schools (FAS). This new body will have 10-15 members appointed by the Secretary of State, drawn from various backgrounds to reflect 'a broad mix of educational and other experience'. Significantly, 'a substantial number of the members will come from outside education, including key appointments from the industrial and commercial worlds'. The new agency will have a chairman (sic) appointed by the Secretary of State, who will also appoint the first chief executive. It will be able to set up regional offices as the number of opted-out schools grows. A new common funding formula will be introduced in 1994 to distribute funds to opted-out schools.

- The White Paper argues that there will need to be a point at which the new Funding Agency takes over responsibility for securing sufficient, suitable school places in the areas of individual LEAs. It proposes that, when more than 10 per cent of either primary or secondary pupils in a council area are educated in grant-maintained schools, the Funding Agency and the LEA will share responsibility for providing a sufficient number of school places. The Funding Agency will take over total responsibility when the proportion of either primary or secondary pupils receiving their education in grant-maintained schools reaches 75 per cent in any given LEA. Indeed, the White Paper argues that some LEAs may wish to shed their responsibility 'well before the 75 per cent "exit point" is reached'.

- LEAs will have a much diminished role. They will be left with limited responsibilities in such areas as special needs, transport and monitoring attendance, and will be able to compete to provide services to grant-maintained schools.
- All secondary schools, whether grant-maintained or under LEA control, will be free to specialise in one or more subjects, in addition to teaching all the core and foundation subjects of the national curriculum. The development of specialisation in a particular curriculum area, such as science, music, modern languages or technology, will depend on the quality of teaching the school is able to offer, and on the range of opportunities to focus on that area. At the same time, the government plans to expand its recent Technology Schools Initiative (the setting up of a network of maintained secondary schools with enhanced technology facilities) and wishes to encourage the growth of grant-maintained and voluntary-aided technology colleges as an extension of the existing 15 CTCs.
- New 'Education Associations' (or 'hit-squad' management teams) comprising five or six members and including retired heads will have powers to take over the running of any schools deemed to be 'at risk'. The job of an education association will be to try to revitalise the school and lead it to grant-maintained status. Alternatively, it can simply recommend that the school be closed. (John Patten has said that he already has 'a little list' of the first schools to be affected by this procedure).
- The National Curriculum Council and the School Examinations and Assessment Council will merge, to be replaced by a powerful single body: the School Curriculum and Assessment Authority.
- Parents of children with special educational needs can expect greater consideration from LEAs; and special schools will be allowed to seek grant-maintained status.
- Firm action will be taken to get rid of 1.5 million surplus school places, a figure that represents, in the words of the White Paper, 'a significant and unacceptable waste of resources'.
- With regard to the problem of school admissions, opted-out schools and LEAs will be encouraged to cooperate wherever possible, although the Education Secretary reserves the right to impose common procedures.
- LEAs will be required to accelerate their review of religious education; and grant-maintained schools will no longer be expected to teach the agreed RE syllabus adopted by their particular LEA. There will be a new classroom emphasis at all levels on spiritual and moral development, and on what constitutes right and wrong.

PARADISE LOST OR PARADISE REGAINED?

The 1992 White Paper will do nothing to facilitate a rebuilding of educational consensus. Quite the reverse is in fact the case. Writing in the *Guardian* on 7 July 1992, former Labour education spokesperson Jack Straw argued that,

> There could have been consensus around both the National Curriculum and LMS if the Tories had then consulted properly on their implementation. But in came City Technology College and opt-out schools, with the ostensible aim of opening up 'choice and opportunity', but with the practical effect of inflaming public opinion about a two-tier service: one side well-funded, the other starved of cash.

It is true that many teachers and parents have come to accept the principle, if not the details, of the national curriculum. It could indeed have secured more widespread support had there been greater consultation with teachers, parents and community representatives. However, many are prepared to concede that it is probably too late to do anything about it now.

There are, however, significant areas of the curriculum where campaigners for progressive reform will continue to make their voice heard. It is clear, for example, that teachers have been intimidated by recent legislation into providing inadequate sex education in schools. The government's White Paper, *The Health of the Nation*, published by Health Secretary Virginia Bottomley in July 1992, claimed to be centrally concerned about teenage pregnancy and the whole issue of sexually-transmitted diseases. Yet the government has axed one health authority family planning clinic in four and has refused to put sex education into the national curriculum.

According to the Education (No 2) Act 1986, it is left to governing bodies to decide whether and how the issue of sex education is approached in their schools. Section 46 of the Act requires that, 'where sex education is given to any registered pupils at a school, it is given in such a manner as to encourage these pupils to have *due regard to moral considerations and the value of family life'*.

This wording was carefully chosen following controversy over the book, *Jenny Lives with Eric and Martin*, which depicts a gay family relationship. Controversy emerged when it was found among the holdings in an inner London teachers' resources centre. The Act was then itself followed by publication of DES Circular No 11/87 and by the notorious Section 28 of the Local Government Act 1988, both of which were designed to restrict classroom discussion of controversial and sensitive issues relating to sexuality.

All of this has, however, created major problems for those seeking to find a place for HIV/AIDS education in the school curriculum. At the end of 1991, Education Secretary Kenneth Clarke neatly side-stepped the whole issue by announcing at a national conference on AIDS that, even in schools with little or no sex education, HIV would still be dealt with as part of the science curriculum 'along with solvent abuse, tobacco, alcohol and other drugs'. Many opponents argued that this prevented AIDS and related issues being placed in a wider context. Clarke, however, responded by citing the 1986 Act and stating that, 'giving governors responsibility for detailed decisions about sex education ensures that schools are accountable to their pupils' parents for what is provided'.[4]

Many are also alarmed by the speed with which the government acted upon one of the key recommendations in the 1992 White Paper. This came with publication at the start of August 1992 of a consultation document aiming to ensure that religious education in schools 'reflects the fact that the religious traditions in Great Britain are in the main Christian'. Launching the document, education minister Baroness Blatch denounced the 'fruit cocktail' approach to religious education, whereby children are taught to understand the key principles of all major faiths. According to Colin Hart of the Christian Institute (and a government supporter),

> There is evidence that in many schools, religious education is not being taught at all. And where it is, Christianity is being watered down. Many of the new syllabuses are full of trendy jargon and multi-faith mish-mash. It is a disgrace. It has to be stamped out.[5]

Additional to all this are problems caused by the many changes made to Key Stage Four of the national curriculum, already discussed in Chapter Five. It seems clear that the concept of a common entitlement curriculum for all is being replaced by that of a differentiated structure whereby, at an early stage, pupils are encouraged to make choices which will affect their future careers. As has already been suggested, the government's new-found desire to vocationalise the secondary-school curriculum, particularly for the 'less able', must be seen against the background of the country's worsening economic situation. Once again, it seems, schools are being expected to prepare youngsters for jobs that do not actually exist. Perhaps, however, it is more a question of socialising teenagers into an acceptance of unemployment, redundancy, low pay and frequent unskilled job changes as inescapable 'facts of life'.

Unemployment in the summer of 1992 again approached the figure of three million that was registered for a number of years in the mid-1980s. Indeed, at this time Britain's jobless figure was rising at a faster rate than anywhere else in Europe or among the world's G7 leading industrial nations. If account is taken of the one million or so people excluded by the 32 changes made to calculation of the count since 1979, the true total was close to four million. Another 450 000 on government-sponsored training and temporary employment schemes were also left out of the total. The fate awaiting the summer's 416 000 school-leavers was therefore singularly grim. Young people were being thrown in to a labour market in which 103 000 16 and 17 year-olds were already unemployed. Of these 'invisible unemployed', 55 000 were without either work or training places.[6]

All governments, whether of Left or Right, find it convenient when necessary to hold schools and teachers responsible for soaring rates of youth unemployment, indeed for the general economic condition of the country. This was the message that James Callaghan and Shirley Williams tried to put across during the 1976-77 Great Debate. The economic dimension is again stressed in the 1992 White Paper. 'School success is critical to our future, for education provides our future work-force and the foundation for the economic development and competitiveness of this country. Without a work-force that is well-educated, we cannot succeed.'[7] It is perhaps worth pointing out that a more cynical view of the government's proposition would hold that if we did value education more highly as a nation, our ailing economy would have difficulty in finding suitable employment for all qualified school-leavers.

The Major government is also very keen that pupils be regularly tested, at 7, 11, 14 and 16, both to assess pupil attainment and to make schools more accountable for the results they achieve. Yet, as far as the latter objective is concerned, it can be argued that publication of new data – examination statistics that make no allowance for intake or catchment area – is a most unsatisfactory way of enabling parents to distinguish between 'good' and 'bad' schools. Desmond Nuttall and

Harvey Goldstein, who teach at the Institute of Education in London, have argued consistently that the main drawback with league tables based on aggregated examination results is that they fail to show how successful a school or college has been in promoting the learning of its students over a given period. In the current jargon, it is the value added by the school which should be used in judging its effectiveness in promoting student achievement.

The second reform around which Jack Straw suggests consensus might have been achieved in the late 1980s involves the handing over to schools of financial responsibilities previously discharged by LEAs. The effects of the introduction of LMS have been the subject of a lengthy research project commissioned by NAHT and carried out by a research team at the School of Education, University of Birmingham.[8] The project continues until September 1993, but initial findings – based on responses to a questionnaire sent to 812 headteachers – were published at the beginning of July 1992. More than three-quarters of the heads surveyed agreed that LMS had required 'too much of their time' to be directed towards administration. LMS apparently meant that, on average, headteachers spent an extra eight hours a week on management tasks, leaving most feeling more remote from classroom matters. Two-thirds said the switch from LEA control of spending had meant an increased workload, which had placed 'unacceptable pressures' upon them.

Despite this, only 15 per cent said they would welcome 'a return to pre-LMS arrangements'. A very large majority of the heads said that local management allowed their schools to make more 'effective' and 'efficient' use of resources. However, there was no agreement over the system's effect on the quality of learning. Because school budgets are now based largely on pupil numbers rather than on funding needs, the survey found that some schools had been disproportionately harmed by changes in their rolls. It was also found that schools had started to employ more teachers on temporary contracts, as they tried to cope with greater fluctuations in funding each year. Significantly for those wishing to promote opting out, almost 75 per cent of heads said they were satisfied with the services provided by their LEAs.

These, then, are the reforms which might have commanded consensus if handled properly. The rest of the 1988 Act and the remainder of the 1992 White Paper are very much politically inspired, chiefly by those on the

Right whose eventual objective is a system or network of independently-managed schools operating to a clearly-defined budget and responsive to the wishes of parents. Yet will the government's reforms have beneficial effects for the vast majority of parents? Will parents get more choice or less as a result of the government's frantic policy making?

WHOSE CHOICE?

In most areas of life, it is the possession of money which provides the citizen with effective choice. This is not strictly true as far as education is concerned, for the 1988 Act set out to provide new types of secondary school within the state sector. Yet this does not mean that effective choice is available to all, since, in the very nature of things, some parents are more knowledgeable, more influential and more articulate than others. They bring to the market-place certain clear advantages. They know how to 'play the system' and win.

Yet the present position is even less equitable still. It is clear that the rhetoric of choice has been employed as a form of camouflage to cover up the reintroduction of selection and privilege. Grant-maintained secondary schools can certainly apply to the Secretary of State to 'change their character', but can also reintroduce selection without going through this time-consuming procedure. Some are already using the interview process to pick the 'brightest' pupils. Some even have a phrase in their new admissions policies stating that pupils must fit in with the ethos of the school. City technology colleges may claim to be 'comprehensive', but they admit that they use the interview process to ensure that new entrants are hard-working, motivated and cooperative. In an area like Wandsworth in South London, which is already experimenting with the idea of each secondary school being able to sell itself by having expertise in a particular curriculum area, it is obvious that two or three schools will attract a disproportionate number of the academic and able, simply because their specialist strength gives them the status of revamped grammar schools.

Wherever there are large numbers of pupils competing for a limited number of places in favoured schools, it is clear that schools choose parents, rather than the other way round. So much is indeed admitted by the Hillgate Group in its 1986 pamphlet, *Whose Schools?*, which advocates the injection of market values into education. Here it is argued that parents should be free to send their children to any school of their choice, while, at the same time, 'schools should have the right to control their own admissions'. To the objection that 'good schools will attract so many applicants that they will no longer be able to contain all the pupils who seek admission', the pamphlet glibly replies that 'there is no reason why schools should not have a right to place an upper limit on their number of admissions'.[9] Even Wandsworth's Chief Education Officer (CEO) Donald Naismith has admitted that he does not know what will happen to those pupils in his borough that no school wants to take.

Indeed, it was reported in the *Guardian* on 4 August 1992 that there is a grant-maintained school in Barnet, North London which is steadily ridding itself of 'difficult' pupils, leaving schools still in the LEA to take them on. Barnet's CEO, Neil Gill, is quoted as saying:

> Under present legislation, many grant-maintained schools have exercised their powers to control their own admissions, so that it is not a question of parents choosing schools, but of schools choosing children. At the end of the day, there may be just one or two LEA schools which will be the 'sink schools' enabling LEAs to fulfil whatever statutory duty they have left. That is the nightmare at the end of this road.

John Patten has so far had very little to say about selection, preferring to leave it to parents to decide. He knows that many Conservative parents are against the whole idea of eleven-plus selection, and simply hopes that, if market forces operate as the government intends they should, influential parents will be able to get their children into the school of their choice. What he dare not acknowledge is that if we return to a divided system of schooling, there are certain to be large numbers of unpopular schools, half-filled with pupils who have no wish to be in them. That is an appalling scenario, the consequences of which could be horrendous. Only the British people can stop it from happening.

NOTES

1. Reported in the *Independent*, 29 July 1992.
2. Department for Education, *Choice and Diversity: A New Framework for Schools*, Cmnd 2021 (HMSO, London, 1992).
3. Ibid, p.5.
4. Reported in the *Times Educational Supplement*, 6 December 1991.
5. Reported in the *Daily Mail*, 4 August 1992.
6. Reported in the *Observer*, 12 July 1992.
7. Department for Education, op cit, p.1.
8. M Arnott, A Bullock and H Thomas, *The Impact of Local Management on Schools: A Source*

Book (School of Education, University of Birmingham, 1992).
9. Hillgate Group, op cit, pp.14,19.

CONCLUSION

The education system of England and Wales has been changed radically in recent years. Further substantial reforms are contained in John Patten's July 1992 White Paper, *Choice and Diversity*. The key intention – and impact – of the Conservatives' reforming measures has been to alter the distribution of power in the education system. In concluding this analysis of the education system transformed, it is this issue of changes in the balance of power which is addressed.

CONFLICTING POWER BASES

Gladstone once wrote that 'the British Constitution presumes, more boldly than any other, the good faith of those who work in it'. A similar remark could be made about the education system that has been known in England and Wales since 1944. The situation was not remedied by the legislation of the 1980s. For the remaining years of this century, the education system will be characterised chiefly by conflicting loyalties and overlapping responsibilities.

With all its faults, the Education Act 1944 endured for over 40 years. Its foundations were not even seriously questioned until the 1980s. This is in stark contrast to the situation in the 1990s. As early as 1992, the Education Reform Act 1988 was felt to require substantial additional legislation. The reason for Patten's important White Paper of July 1992 is that many radical provisions in the 1988 Act are either unworkable or inadequate. Yet the White Paper itself leaves many key questions unanswered.

The 1988 Act and the 1992 White Paper both assume that, despite the ambiguity of their relationship, headteachers and governors will be able to work together quite amicably. Yet when the relationship breaks down, as happened in spring 1992 at grant-maintained Stratford School in Newham, East London, it is wholly unclear how problems can be resolved without causing irreparable damage to pupils' academic progress. The government is clearly determined that school governing bodies should wield very great power in order, partly, to curb the autonomy of teachers. However, this determination is based on the unproven assumption that all governors will act in the interests of all pupils at all times.

Similarly, difficulties arise from the 1989 high court decision that the London Borough of Bromley be required to admit children from outside the borough, instead of giving automatic priority to its own children. The problems created by this judgment have been exacerbated by growing numbers of grant-maintained schools in the borough, each of which has its own idiosyncratic admissions policy. The government has not been prepared to introduce legislation to overturn the high court judgment, and now seems to be pinning all its hopes on a new spirit of cooperation between LEAs and grant-maintained schools. On this matter, the Patten White Paper simply states that LEAs and opted-out schools should consider setting up joint arrangements in order to reduce delay and uncertainty for parents.

INCREASED POWER AT THE CENTRE

On many occasions, the government's only solution to problems created by its own reforms has been to increase the power of the Secretary of State. The result is an education system which was described by the education correspondent of the *Observer* on 2 August 1992 as 'one of the most centralised, undemocratic and bureaucratic education systems in the Western world'.

In future, the powers of elected LEAs will increasingly be taken over by an unaccountable education quango (the FAS). The Education Secretary will have the power to remove governors of schools that run into difficulties, to force closure on schools with falling rolls, to force expansion on other schools, and to decide whether or not a secondary school can 'change its character' and bring back the eleven-plus. Curriculum and assessment policies will also be decided by a new quango (the SCAA), which will be staffed by people hand-picked by government on ideological grounds. They will be monitored by new teams of inexperienced inspectors whose chief qualification will be that they have submitted the cheapest tenders. All of this is, moreover, claimed to operate in the cause of allowing unfettered market forces to function without interference by elected bodies or mediating institutions.

DISREGARD OF PROFESSIONAL OPINION

The Education Act 1944 was the product of nearly three years' consultation. It was legislated by a wartime coalition government which allowed a number of different viewpoints to be expressed. By contrast, the Thatcher and Major administrations have forced educational reform through parliament at speed, without adequate consultation, and without even seeking to create consensus for their plans. This is perhaps the single greatest tragedy of the past 13 years.

It demonstrates a marked contempt for professional opinion and experience. All too often, teachers have been made scapegoats for the government's own failings. Their advice is rarely heeded. The fact that children in schools have not suffered unduly from transformation of the eductaion system since 1979 is a substantial tribute to the teachers of this country.

APPENDICES

Appendix 1: Post-war administrations, 1945-1992

Party	Date formed	Prime Minister
Labour	July 1945	Clement Attlee
Conservative	October 1951	Winston Churchill
Conservative	May 1955	Sir Anthony Eden
Conservative	January 1957	Harold Macmillan
Conservative	October 1963	Sir Alec Douglas-Home
Labour	October 1964	Harold Wilson
Conservative	June 1970	Edward Heath
Labour	March 1974	Harold Wilson
Labour	April 1976	James Callaghan
Conservative	May 1979	Margaret Thatcher
Conservative	November 1990	John Major

Note: Only dates on which a change of prime minister took place are recorded. General elections which produced no change of prime minister – those of 1950, 1959, 1966, October 1974, 1983, 1987 and 1992 – do not therefore feature here.

Appendix 2: Ministers of Education 1945-64, Secretaries of State for Education and Science 1964-92, and Secretary of State for Education 1992.

	Date on which took office
Ellen Wilkinson	July 1945
George Tomlinson	February 1947
Florence Horsbrugh	November 1951
Sir David Eccles	October 1954
Viscount Hailsham	January 1957
Geoffrey Lloyd	September 1957
Sir David Eccles	October 1959
Sir Edward Boyle	July 1962
Quintin Hogg	April 1964
Michael Stewart	October 1964
Anthony Crosland	January 1965
Patrick Gordon-Walker	August 1967
Edward Short	April 1968
Margaret Thatcher	June 1970
Reginald Prentice	March 1974
Fred Mulley	June 1975
Shirley Williams	September 1976
Mark Carlisle	May 1979
Sir Keith Joseph	September 1981
Kenneth Baker	May 1986
John MacGregor	July 1989
Kenneth Clarke	November 1990
John Patten	April 1992

Notes: 1. In April 1964 the Ministry of Education was reorganised, and became the Department of Education and Science (DES). The Education Minister became the Secretary of State for Education and Science. In April 1992, the DES became the Department for Education (DFE). The office-holder became the Secretary of State for Education.
2. Viscount Hailsham and Quinton Hogg are one and the same person.

A BRIEF GUIDE TO FURTHER READING

The best guides to recent reform of the education system are:

Brown P and H Lauder (eds), *Education for Economic Survival: From Fordism to Post-Fordism* (Routledge, London, 1991)

Chitty C, *Towards a new Education System: The Victory of the New Right?* (Falmer Press, Lewes, 1989)

Chitty C (ed), *Post-Sixteen Education: Studies in Access and Achievement* (Kogan Page, London, 1991)

Flude M and M Hammer (eds), *The Education Reform Act, 1988: Its Origins and Implications* (Falmer Press, Lewes, 1990)

Green A, *Education and State Formation: The Rise of Education Systems in England, France and the USA* (Macmillan, London, 1990)

Hillcole Group, *Changing the Future: Redprint for Education* (Tufnell Press, London, 1991)

Jones K, *Right Turn: The Conservative Revolution in Education* (Hutchinson Radius, London, 1989)

Jones K (ed), *English and the National Curriculum: Cox's Revolution?* (Kogan Page in association with the Institute of Education, University of London, London, 1992)

Lawton D, *Education, Culture and the National Curriculum* (Hodder and Stoughton, London, 1989)

Lowe R (ed), *The Changing Secondary School* (Falmer Press, Lewes, 1989)

Maclure S, *Education Re-Formed: A Guide to the Education Reform Act 1988* (Hodder and Stoughton, London, 1988)

Ranson S, *The Politics of Reorganising Schools* (Unwin Hyman, London, 1990)

Rattansi A and D Reeder (eds), *Rethinking Radical Education* (Lawrence and Wishart, London, 1992)

Riley J (ed), *The National Curriculum and the Primary School: Springboard or Straitjacket?* (Kogan Paul in association with the Institute of Education, University of London, London, 1992)

Simon B, *What Future for Education?* (Lawrence and Wishart, London, 1991)

INDEX